ECONOMIC NATIONALISM
AND STABILITY

ECONOMIC NATIONALISM AND STABILITY

George Macesich

PRAEGER SPECIAL STUDIES • PRAEGER SCIENTIFIC

New York • Philadelphia • Eastbourne, UK
Toronto • Hong Kong • Tokyo • Sydney

Library of Congress Cataloging-in-Publication Data

Macesich, George, 1927-
    Economic nationalism and stability.

    Includes bibliographies and index.
    1. Developing countries—Economic policy.
2. Economic stabilization—Developing countries.
3. Economic policy. 4. Nationalism. I. Title.
HC59.7.M2112 1985   338.9'009172'4   85-12342
ISBN 0-03-005748-5

Published in 1985 by Praeger Publishers
CBS Educational and Professional Publishing, a Division of CBS Inc.
521 Fifth Avenue, New York, NY 10175 USA

© 1985 by Praeger Publishers

56789 052 987654321

Printed in the United States of America on acid-free paper

INTERNATIONAL OFFICES

Orders from outside the United States should be sent to the appropriate address listed below. Orders from areas not listed below should be placed through CBS International Publishing, 383 Madison Ave., New York, NY 10175 USA

Australia, New Zealand

Holt Saunders, Pty, Ltd., 9 Waltham St., Artarmon, N.S.W. 2064, Sydney, Australia

Canada

Holt, Rinehart & Winston of Canada, 55 Horner Ave., Toronto, Ontario, Canada M8Z 4X6

Europe, the Middle East, & Africa

Holt Saunders, Ltd., 1 St. Anne's Road, Eastbourne, East Sussex, England BN21 3UN

Japan

Holt Saunders, Ltd., Ichibancho Central Building, 22-1 Ichibancho, 3rd Floor, Chiyodaku, Tokyo, Japan

Hong Kong, Southeast Asia

Holt-Saunders Asia, Ltd., 10 Fl, Intercontinental Plaza, 94 Granville Road, Tsim Sha Tsui East, Kowloon, Hong Kong

Manuscript submissions should be sent to the Editorial Director, Praeger Publishers, 521 Fifth Avenue, New York, NY 10175 USA

In Memory of

My Uncle

Milić Macesich, I

PREFACE

This study examines economic nationalism and stability primarily in emerging Third World nations. The basic framework is the theory of economic nationalism. Monetary theory and policy are drawn upon and the evidence provided by recent studies, history, and economic experience of several countries is examined.

The study draws especially on the work of the late Harry G. Johnson and on economic nationalism. This book considers and extends the implications of economic nationalism for emerging Third World nations and particularly for their monetary and financial stability.

The book examines and surveys the antecedents of ideas that form and shape contemporary economic nationalism. At the same time it discusses the constraints within which such a policy operates. Emerging nations may well use economic nationalism as an integrative force and as a propellant to accelerate economic development. Thanks to growing world interdependence, however, such a policy may also impose serious costs, including monetary instability on the country. It may be that nationalism per se has outgrown its usefulness to the nation-state.

In view of the serious side effects of economic nationalism, this study recommends a cosmopolitan alternative and a system of well-defined guides within lawful policy systems that constrains bureaucracies and elites from the discretionary exercise of power, especially in the monetary-financial areas. The more closely constrained their actions are by rules or performance criteria, the less their power and prestige and the less will their interests coalesce with promoting the excess "production" of nationalism. This is important since economic nationalism may block economic growth so that it becomes necessary to resort to even more extreme nationalistic sentiment and policy as the only means available to maintain the illusion of economic development.

The book is directed to the general economist, political scientist, international affairs specialist, and layman with an interest in the issues of economic nationalism and stability. I am indebted to many colleagues with whom I have discussed one aspect or another of this study over the years. These include especially the late Harry G. Johnson, Marshall R. Colberg, Walter Macesich, Jr., Dimitrije Dimitrijević, Branimir M. Janković, Anna J. Schwartz, Rikard Lang, Dragomir Vojnić, and Ljubisav Marković. I would also like to express appreciation to Clydeyne Nelson for efficient and helpful typing services.

CONTENTS

ECONOMIC NATIONALISM
AND STABILITY

1

ECONOMIC NATIONALISM AND EMERGING NATIONS

THE ESSENCE OF NATIONALISM

This study focuses on economic nationalism. It is therefore useful to consider the essence of nationalism, which scientific analysis has cast up as a way of coming to grips with the complexities of the subject at hand.[1]

Nationalism is derived from "nation," which itself has roots in the Latin *natio*, signifying birth. It has been taken to mean a social grouping with or without ties of blood. In the Middle Ages the term *natio villae* was used to designate a kinship in the village. Indeed later in the period students at the University of Paris were divided into "nations" according to their places of birth. Later the term "nation" was applied to the population of a country without regard for racial unity. By the late eighteenth century the term "nation" began to be used abstractly and indeed interchangeably with "country."

Currently, scholars distinguish a nation from a race, a state, or a language. In particular the emphasis is placed on a common political sentiment. The political term "nation" is used by some scholars as designating a people that "has attained to state organization." Hans Kohn, for instance, places the emphasis on the "the political doctrine of sovereignty" as the principal characteristic of modern nations.[2] In effect, the contemporary connotation of "nation" is political.

The concept of "nationalism" is even less precise.[3] It can be taken to mean the historical process by which nationalities become political units or modern national states constructed out of tribes and empires.

1

It can be taken to mean the theory, principle, or ideal implicit in the actual historical process. It can be taken to mean the activity of a political party, thereby combining the historical process and political theory. It can be taken to mean a condition of the mind among the members constituting the nationality, sharing commitment to the ideal of one's own national state and/or mission of the national state. It is as Kohn suggests, "first and foremost a state of mind, an act of consciousness."

Some scholars argue that the concept of nationalism is best understood by the social psychologist. It is defined by some as the "self-consciousness" of a nation and by others as an "intolerant and aggressive instinct." Still others describe nationalism as a way of manifesting national spirit: history, traditions, language, and in its abstract form as an idea controlling the life and actions of a nation.

The essence of nationalism with which many scholars agree is that it reflects social mobilization whereby the commitment of an individual is transferred from the local to the national level.[4] On this view the individual becomes aware that his interests go beyond his local community to the national level. In effect, the individual turns from the local level to a national community for economic status, political loyalty, social dependence, cultural form, and psychological drive. Though it may differ from country to country in details, in emphasis and in time, this sort of social mobilization is the essence of nationalism.

In terms of economic policy, nationalism typically involves an ideological preference for a number of goals. These include as much self-sufficiency as possible, public ownership and public enterprise in key economic sectors, and/or intensive regulation and control of private and domestic and foreign enterprise. In general, discrimination in favor of nationals is carried on as a matter of policy. This discrimination, however, is not uniform in terms of nationals. There is a bias in favor of the ruling elite and bureaucracy. To be sure this may also be an investment in the creation and maintenance of a class deemed necessary to the construction and perpetuation of a viable national state for the common good.

There may also be reasons other than economic nationalism why some governments pursue the above policies. Socialists, for instance, are not necessarily nationalists yet they may prefer a collective economy for ideological reasons. Governments may also see external economies to be realized in pursuing protective trade measures on behalf of the industries of their nationals. The consequences, unfortunately, may be the same as the pursuit of parochial nationalist policies. This study, however, focuses on economic nationalism and the implications of such policies, particularly for emerging countries.[5]

PROSPECTS FOR NATIONALISM

What are the prospects for nationalism? It can be viewed as a historical movement that has within it the seeds of its own destruction. The nation-state and the nationalism that provides the glue to hold it together are undergoing change thanks to growing world economic, political, social, and technological interpendence. Thus it may be that nationalism per se has outgrown its usefulness to the nation-state. Thanks to the initiative of their leadership, emerging nations have copied and attempted to make their own an antiquated and obsolete Euro-American model for nation-building. Though its surface manifestations continue to exist, the fundamental forces, conditions, and circumstances that made nationalism a powerful force for nation-building in the past no longer exist in their previous form and strength. Indeed, those who wrap themselves up in the skirts of nationalism are living in the dangerous past.

The growing world economic, political, social, and technological interdependence has undermined the authority of the nation-state. Thus the nation-state can no longer guarantee its nationals against the threat of external aggression with the same assurance that it did for centuries in the past. This had been the nation-state's primary role. Nationalism is simply ineffective as a political concept when no government, large or small, can protect itself against nuclear attack.

Domestic and foreign policies of nation-states can no longer be as sharply separated as in former years. Indeed these policies more often than not tend to merge and become dependent upon one another. There is an increased sense of international awareness in such problems as monetary policy, economics, pollution, control of disease, air travel, traffic in drugs, and related problems. At best national efforts alone yield limited results. National problems tend to yield more and more to international solutions.

In effect, the reality, which is working its way in the world as the capacity for mutual destruction has increased since World War II, is that nations are becoming a little less interested in settling their disputes by force of arms and a little more interested in cooperating in limited fields because it is in their selfish interest to do so. To be sure, scholars have known for generations and even centuries that nations must cooperate in many fields to avoid damage to their own people. Scattered evidence suggests that governments are gradually adjusting to this view. In the process nationalism is being undermined by a new internationalism, or transnationalism, or, better still, cosmopolitanism.

This process of decay evident in nationalism is nevertheless a very slow one indeed. Nationalism continues to show vigor. The sense of national identity remains important. In confrontation with such other isms as capitalism, socialism, fascism, and communism, nationalism thus far is demonstrably more resilient as a historical movement. In fact, many of the isms make it only when identified with nationalism. Each nation, no matter what its size, is jealous of its sovereignty and does not intend to sacrifice even a small portion of its independence for the promised advantages of international cooperation. For such nations nationalism of the Euro-American model is essential to assure what they regard as freedom of decision and action. They prefer self-government with all its dangers to servitude in tranquillity. They prefer to be governed by their own kind than by foreign administrators, no matter how efficient. Nationalism remains the mainspring of mass action. The mental gymnastics required to justify nationalism in an interdependent world are all too evident.[6]

A COSMOPOLITAN ALTERNATIVE

The problem in so many countries lies in economies that have not fulfilled the hopes of their citizens. During the first quarter-century after World War II, decolonization created new nations and new hopes. Membership in the United Nations rose from 51 to 158. The former colonies graduated in an era when both Western and Eastern economies were enjoying what seemed to be an endless growth cycle. The momentum of rebuilding war-shattered economies carried the former Axis and Allied powers into an unusual era of growth and citizens' hope. For the new leaders of new nations, there was a rich menu of choices to participate in the banquet.

They could join the American or West European economic spheres —trade, aid, loans, and educational opportunities. Or they could sample the Soviet promise, the more Spartan wave of the future. Later they could choose the heretical Chinese version of Marxist aid—perhaps a Tanzam railway—if they suspected Moscow's brand of being just another version of white imperialism. Or, they could listen for a higher bid from Nationalist China (Taiwan)—perhaps ingenious agricultural aid that produced not one, not two, but three rice crops a year.

Such nonaligned countries as Guinea, Indonesia, Ghana, Egypt, and Yugoslavia experimented with the Soviet-brand product, then rejected it. India alternately considered a post-Stalinist model then a Galbraithean interventionist model. Yugoslavia developed its own unique market-oriented worker-management model.

In a few Third World nations, rising economies helped to satisfy rising expectations. For most, however, there was only the wild rise and fall of world commodity prices, or the showplace bid project East or West that never seemed to launch the local society into self-sustaining growth. They never reached the so-called take-off stage.

With disappointment came coups. These served to increase the desire on the part of the "elite" or "establishment" in many countries to attempt to insulate themselves from external influences and from the dangers of votes, electoral or parliamentary, that might express dissatisfaction with the course of economic affairs. Attempts to aid free trade and internal democracy in a number of these countries—sometimes by helping exiled leaders committed to popular rule; sometimes by withholding aid, downgrading diplomatic recognition, and/or speaking out against offenders—have seldom worked. In fact, thanks to skillful propaganda the unrest and protest in many of these nations has on occasion turned into anti-Americanism. The Soviet Union for its part has not done much better in registering notable success in its dealings with these countries.

What then are the answers, if any? It is not very useful not to put forward one's views. This study argues that policies promoting economic nationalism as a means for promoting development have miscarried. For the most part these policies have not been able to solve the problems of development in emerging nations. They have, as expected, served well to cultivate and promote the interests and prosperity of the elite and bureaucracy in many countries. To be sure, each country has its own particular problems and economic structure toward which its economic policy is directed. As a consequence there are important differences among nations with respect to economic policy. This study makes a point of recognizing these differences while at the same time stressing similarities.

What beckons are more cosmopolitan and international economic policies that emphasize the entrepreneurial competitive market-oriented incentive systems practiced in economically successful nation-states. Many of the leaders of emerging nations, whether democratic, authoritarian, or totalitarian, received their education abroad. Most are well aware of the implications of the progress of the world's developed nations. Modernization to them does mean the necessity of learning more about the results of the developed world's technical efficiency.

They were observant and good students. They saw how appeals to tradition solidified national sentiment, how devotion to the state was made the citizen's prime responsibility, how poets sang about the glory of the fatherland, and how patriots regretted that they had but one life to lose for their own country. They are familiar with Rousseau's social contract, with Montesquieu's analysis of the spirit of legal institutions, and Alexander Hamilton's project of a national economy. They know how Bismarck unified the German national state, how Mazzini, Garibaldi, and Cavour stimulated Italian unity, how Marx and Lenin proposed to change the world, and the vision of Keynes.

Once they returned home, this elite with much charisma and on occasion with political genius gave direction to the nationalism, including economic nationalism, of their emerging countries. They wanted liberation from the bonds of imperialism, but at the same time they would construct their new nation-states in the image of the developed nation-states. They would accept economic modernization but maintain their ancient cultural heritage. They would superimpose industrialism upon their predominantly agrarian economies while introducing agricultural reforms. They were torn between the old and new. This dilemma explains in part the unevenness of development in emerging nations, the constant crises, the spasmodic changes in leadership, and the air of discord and dissension. The pursuit of policies promoting economic nationalism are not always helpful and are often counterproductive.

This is a familiar story through which many of the world's developed nations passed more than two centuries ago. The differences are that today the world is much more integrated, and in today's emerging nations the experience is telescoped and more rapid. There is thus less chance for the successful pursuit of economic nationalism than in the earlier period. A competent and patient political leadership recognizes that nation-states that have given their peoples hope and rising standards are more apt to end up becoming modern democratic states. Indeed, the spirit of enterprise, independent judgment, desire for progress and change, knowledge of the world, and improved education are ingredients essential to these states. These are the very ingredients often lacking in a policy of economic nationalism. They are also the ingredients that should be promoted and cultivated by political and economic leaders of even one-party states with a genuine long-term interest in the development of their countries.

In fact, China in 1984 began to restructure its economic system radically. The Central Committee, in a 16,000-word report, decided to transform the Chinese economy from a centrally planned system like that of the Soviet Union to a more flexible one similar to Hungary or Yugoslavia. Several years ago, China reformed its agriculture by replacing the collectivized communes with family farm units, which sharply boosted food output and rural incomes.

Central controls, the report says, impede innovation, foster waste, and distort output. The new program would restrict central planning, expand the authority of enterprises over wages, prices, and product, and rely much more on the market and competition to guide production and pricing. A wider spread in wages would be encouraged to reward diligence, productivity, and skill.

The report recognizes that the reform is a sharp break with the past and that it is complex and cannot be achieved "at one stroke." Getting rid of consumer subsidies, adjusting prices and wages, and avoiding inflation or undue unemployment will be difficult and will risk serious social dislocation and discontent. Even if pursued vigorously the reform will take time.

This is a bold and realistic step. Leaders of the Soviet Union, which also suffers for the same reasons from slow growth, inefficiency, low quality, and lack of innovation in industry and agriculture, have recognized the problems for some years but have done little beyond exhortation and palliatives. Why can China move to reform its economy while the Soviet Union cannot? In both cases, one can assume the bureaucrats and party officials resist changes bound to threaten their positions and perquisites. Moreover, in the Soviet Union they have been entrenching themselves at least since Stalin. In 1964 Nikita S. Khrushchev was ousted mainly because these groups felt threatened. In China, however, both the government and party were so disrupted by the Cultural Revolution under Mao Tse-tung that they had not been able to dig in solidly.

Similarly, in Yugoslavia following the 1948 break with the Soviet Union the country's leadership was able to break out on its own course of development. To be sure, it was some years before the country managed to put together a workable model of development. In fact, the process of developing such a model is still incomplete.

In both China and Yugoslavia the key factor is the character of the leadership. In China it is Deng Xiaoping. In Yugoslavia it was Josef Broz Tito. Both have shown the ability to recognize and diagnose their country's economic problems, to think freshly and pragmatically about how to cope with them, and to exercise the political skill and patience to build a political base for radical measures. Both have that rare combination, essential for major leadership, of strategic vision and practical action. The Soviet Union thus far has not produced such leaders.

Ironically, the Soviet Union already depends on a form of private entrepreneurship to meet a growing shortage of fruit, vegetables, and other produce. Private plots in the country, for example, provide half of some types of produce, although they occupy only a fraction of the land area of state and collective farms. The country has yet to move away from cumbersome central economic planning. Unlike the late Yuri Andropov, his successor, the late Konstantin Chernenko, was a firm adherent of state central planning—siding with the bureaucracy in the ongoing debate over the path the country's economy should take.

For better, or—quite possibly—for worse, world leadership and elites including most in emerging countries share a common intellectual heritage. This heritage includes mercantilist, classical, neoclassical, Marxian, Keynesian, and Monetarist economic doctrines. Many of these doctrines are as relevant to developed and emerging countries today as they were in the past. They merit our attention. For this reason this study surveys the thoughts of economists and others by drawing upon these doctrines for the historical and theoretical insights they provide on economic nationalism.

A survey of these doctrines and ideas underscores important differences in their approaches and methods toward economic nationalism and government intervention into economic affairs. The emerging countries have indeed a rich menu from which to select. Not all of the available selections, however, are equally healthy for a country's economy and its development. Some selections are very unhealthy indeed.

There are, moreover, constraints to what a country can do in its promotion of economic nationalism. As this study underscores, these constraints are multidimensional and include cultural, economic, monetary, and political elements. They are not simply internal to the country. More importantly they are also external. Their net effects are to reduce a nationalist government's room to maneuver in promoting a policy of economic nationalism regardless of the skill and determination of its political leadership. What a country can do in today's interdependent world depends only in part on its size, location, resources, and the ethnic bases for its nationalism.

Urging cosmopolitan and less government interventionist economic policies on emerging nations and others in an interdependent world is neither hypocritical nor does it necessarily mean accepting one or the other programs of superpowers as some argue.[7] On the contrary, it is a recognition of contemporary world reality and the shortcomings of parochial nationalist economic policies.

NOTES

1. A useful discussion of nationalism in English is presented in Louis L. Snyder, *Varieties of Nationalism: A Comparative Study* (Hinsdale, Ill.: The Dryden Press, 1976); K. W. Deutch, *Nationalism and Social Communication: An Inquiry into the Foundations of Nationality* (New York: John Wiley, 1953); E. H. Carr, *Nationalism and After* (New York: Macmillan, 1945); S. W. Baron, *Modern Nationalism and Religion* (New York: Harper, 1947); L. W. Doob, *Patriotism and Nationalism: Their Psychological Foundations* (New Haven, Conn.: Yale University Press, 1964); C. J. H. Hayes, *The Historical Evolution of Modern Nationalism* (New York: R. R. Smith, 1931); F. O. Hertz, *Nationality in History and Politics* (New York: Oxford University Press, 1944); H. Kohn, *The Idea of Nationalism* (New York: Macmillan, 1944); F. Znaniecki, *Modern Nationalities: A Sociological Study* (Urbana: University of Illinois Press, 1952); B. C. Shafer, *Faces of Nationalism* (New York: Harcourt Brace Jovanovich, 1972); Harry G. Johnson, ed., *Economic Nationalism in Old and New States* (Chicago: University of Chicago Press, 1967); K. E. Deutsch and W. J. Poltz, eds., *Nation-Building* (New York: Atherton, 1963); E. M. Earle, ed., *Nationalism and Internationalism: Essays Inscribed to Carlton J. A. Hayes* (New York: Columbia University Press, 1950); A. Eban, *The Tide of Nationalism* (New York: Horizon Press, 1959); H. A. Gibbons, *Nationalism and Internationalism* (New York: Stokes, 1930); G. P. Gooch, *Nationalism* (New York: Harcourt Brace and Howe, 1920); F. H. Hinsley, *Nationalism and the International System* (London: Hodder and Staughton, 1973); O. Jaszi, *The Dissolution of the Habsburg Monarchy* (Chicago: University of Chicago Press, 1929); L. L. Snyder, *The Dynamics of Nationalism* (Princeton, N.J.: Van Nostrand, 1964).

2. Kohn, *The Idea of Nationalism.*

3. See, for instance, Hayes, *The Historical Evolution of Modern Nationalism.*

4. Snyder (in *Varieties of Nationalism*, p. 25) defines nationalism as

that sentiment of a group or body of people living within a compact or noncontiguous territory, using a language or related dialects as a vehicle for common thoughts and feelings, holding a common religious belief, possessing common institutions, traditions and customs acquired and transmitted during the course of common history, venerating national heroes, and cherishing a common will for social homogeniety.

In any given situation one or more of these elements may be absent, as Snyder points out, without affecting the validity of the definition.

5. In the post-World War II period, events all over the world have moved swiftly to bring new troubles and to make old ones harder to manage. The new

ones sprang up chiefly in those areas variously called developing, underprivileged, colonial, or emerging. They ranged in extent from the Western Hemisphere to the East, Near and Far, and in intensity from protest to revolt against things as they were (and some argue still are), the established order, and former colonial powers. Indeed, the term "Third World" is intended to distinguish these developing nation-states, many of them small, from two groups of technologically advanced nations: the so-called Western nations, largely influenced by the United States, and the Soviet Socialist nations, influenced by the Soviet Union. Communist China, which used to be classified as a Third World country, might now be more accurately described as a fourth power in the balance of nations. See George Macesich, *The International Monetary Economy and the Third World* (New York: Praeger, 1981).

6. See, for instance, Dudley Seers, *The Political Economy of Nationalism* (Oxford: Oxford University Press, 1983).

7. Ibid., p. 12.

2

ECONOMIC IMPLICATIONS

The fundamental framework from which this study draws economic implications of nationalism is based on the work of Harry G. Johnson, Albert Breton, Anthony Downs, Gary S. Becker, and my own earlier work on economic policies in several countries.[1] It also benefits from conversations that I had with Harry G. Johnson in the early 1960s on various topics dealing with the economics of nationalism.

Downs argues that political parties attempt to maximize the gains from political office by catering to the tastes and preferences of voters. In a multiparty democratic society, political parties remain in office only by satisfying these tastes and preferences for various types and amounts of government programs. In effect, political power is exchanged for desired policies in a political transaction between party and electorate.

The critical element in Downs's hypothesis is the cost of acquiring information. He uses this cost to explain reliance on persuasion in arriving at political decisions, the inequality of political influence, the role of ideology, electoral apathy, and the bias in democratic government toward serving producer rather than consumer interests.

Breton's analysis of economic nationalism identifies nationality with ownership by nationals of various types of property and considers such nationality as a type of collective consumption capital that yields an income of utility and can be invested in by spending public funds in the acquisition of such capital. From these assumptions he derives a number of testable propositions about nationalism.

These propositions about nationalism imply, among other things, that nationalist policy is primarily concerned with redistributing rather than increasing income. The redistribution, moreover, is from the working class to the middle class. As a result, there will be a tendency to resort to confiscation rather than purchase when the working class is poor. Since manufacturing jobs and ownership are preferred by the middle class, nationalism will tend to favor investment in national manufacturing. Given its collective nature, nationalism will strike a particularly responsive chord from socialists. Furthermore, the blossoming and appeal of nationalism will be closely associated with the rise of new middle classes who have difficulty in finding suitable career opportunities.

Johnson develops and extends Downs's cost of information regarding voter preferences and extends the concept from Downs's established democracies to include emerging countries. Thus, the main obstacle to efficiency in the exchange between political parties and their electorate stems from ignorance on both sides about prospective gains from policies offered and cost of acquiring the information necessary to make the exchange efficient. This obstacle forces the political party to depend for its information about voter preferences on pressure groups, lobbyists, and communications media. One consequence of this dependence is to give political parties a strong incentive to gain control over communications media as a means of establishing control over the country. Indeed, the recent push by emerging countries for a "New Information Order" is consistent with Johnson's hypothesis.

Given that the average voter is motivated by his own rational self-interest not to acquire much information about policies of political parties and the consequences for his economic welfare—for the reason that whether well informed or not he will have negligible influence on which party is elected—ideology steps in to play a key role in political affairs. Ideology simplifies a political party's problem of communicating with its electorate. Its policies can be summarized in symbolism or slogans. Thus the voter's problem is also simplified since he can vote by ideology instead of investing his time in evaluating each party's record and promises on a whole range of particular policy issues. As a result, parties will tend for the most part to compete through ideologies.

In established democracies, according to our above sources, the type of party system that emerges will depend on a variety of features, including the distribution among voters of ideological preferences, type of election system (whether by proportional representation or by plurality), and geographical distribution of voter preferences. Thus proportionality will tend to foster a multiplicity of ideologically differentiated parties. Plurality elections will tend to promote a two-party system, except where ideological differences are associated with geographical region. Actual policy in a multiparty system will tend to present a compromise among ideologies owing to the necessity of forming coalitions to obtain power. In two-party systems the relation of party ideologies will be determined by the distribution of voter preferences for ideologies. Thus if the distribution of voter preference for ideology is unimodal, there will be a grouping around a central ideological position and party ideologies will not differ significantly. On the other hand, if voter preferences are multimodal, then voter preferences that will group around two or more ideological positions become very important. If a party departs too significantly from its ideological position it may alienate its constituents, who will tend not to vote. Or worse, if party ideologies are significantly differentiated the country itself will tend to be politically unstable and ripe for disintegration.

Matters are somewhat different when democracy is not well established. The incentive is for a political party to attempt to create a comprehensive and preclusive ideology to enable it to enjoy exclusive control of government. Emerging countries, observes Johnson, are particularly susceptible on this score. This is reinforced by the fact that in emerging countries a change in government is likely to impose significant costs on those who have to wait for political office by contrast with holding power and political office permanently. To be sure, even in developed democracies the change of office by political parties tends to be wasteful. The economic and sociopolitical system in such countries tends to reabsorb ousted political office holders without imposing great private losses on them. Consequently, the ability of the economic and sociopolitical system not to impose undue losses on political losers as well as the acceptance of the rules of the game of democracies and their principles are important in cultivating workable democracies.

Indeed it is nationalistic feeling that provides a foundation for the establishment of a preclusive ideology as a prerequisite for a single-party government. Johnson calls attention to the connection between the stridency of nationalism in emerging countries and their propensity to establish a one-party government. However, even where the two-party system is maintained, the competition in ideology would tend to make both parties stress nationalism and nationalist policies if there were widespread nationalist sentiment among the electorate. Johnson succinctly observes that only if there is sharp division of voter preferences, with some voters envisaging serious disadvantages, would there be significant political division on the issues and the likelihood that the political stability would be threatened.

Downs, moreover, underscores that the working of political democracy will display a certain asymmetry between producer and consumer interests. The concentration will be on producer interests and often at the expense of those of the consumer. Johnson extends this observation to nationalism and nationalist policies. Since producer costs can be spread thinly over a mass of consumers, nationalist policies win political support more readily by promoting producer interests even though the net benefits, taking consumers and producers together, tend to be negative.

Our theoretical framework thus far outlines the working of political democracy and party government, integrating nationalism in emerging countries into the framework. We can draw on Becker's work on racial discrimination and Johnson's interpretation to consider nationalism as a cultivated preference and call it a "taste for nationalism." This is identical with Becker's concept of "taste for discrimination." That is, people who discriminate actually are willing to give up pecuniary returns for doing so in return for the nonpecuniary or psychic income derived from avoiding the group discriminated against. In Becker's study the group discriminated against were Negroes in the United States. Johnson substitutes "taste for nationalism" for Becker's "taste for discrimination." Accordingly, the taste for nationalism attaches utility to certain jobs or certain property owned by members of the national group, even though pecuniary returns are foregone as a result of exercising such tastes.

The types of property and jobs to which such utility is attached are obviously the prestige jobs and socially significant property. These include, for example, literary and cultural activities. Others include political and economic activities and properties with high prestige and incomes. The nationalist utility attached to the various properties, jobs, and cultural and other activities is derived internally from an emerging country's colonial era and/or externally by observing what takes place in more developed countries.

Nationalism is a collective consumption good or public good whereby its consumption by one individual does not exclude its consumption by others. The problem is one of determining the optimum amount of nationalism to supply. The specific benefits of nationalism obviously go to those select nationals who acquire offices and/or property rights in which nationalism invests. This would include the bureaucracy, elite, and producer interests. Thanks to the desire on the part of cultural, linguistic, and communication interests to cultivate monopoly power, they are natural beneficiaries of a policy of economic nationalism. All of these interests are vulnerable to foreign competition.

Since everyone in the national state must consume the same quantity and quality of the public "nationalism" good, even though their preferences and tax payments for the good may vary, it is not surprising that there is considerable controversy on the output (and resource input) of public goods by the nation-state. Some consumers want more and some less. Few will agree that the optimal quantity is truly optimal.[2]

As we have noted, collective decisions in political markets are complex. People can communicate their desires for public goods through voting behavior. Still, what a consumer-voter desires in a political market may be significantly different from what he or she ultimately receives. The correlation between a voter's choice and the expected outcome may be very weak. Efficient political decisions tend to affect everyone in the community, unlike decisions in a private market, which affect primarily the consumer and supplier of a given product or service.

Moreover, if the demand for nationalism as a "club good" by the elite and bureaucracy is added to the demand by the general population for nationalism as a public good, it is likely that there will be an overproduction of nationalism. This will tend to allocate too many resources for the creation and preservation of the nation-state, including a formidable bureaucracy and military.

It is thus imperative that the bureaucracy and elite be discouraged and indeed constrained from the use of nationalism to maximize their returns and advantages. One way is to structure the incentive system so as to prevent or, at best, limit the abuse of their authority. The method this study recommends is a system of well-defined guides within lawful policy systems. In effect, it argues for a system of rules that constrains the bureaucrasies and elites from the discretionary exercise of power. The more closely constrained the actions are by rules or performance criteria, the less their power and prestige and the less will their interests coalesce with promoting the excess production of nationalism.

As a public good, economic nationalism in particular appeals to the elite and bureaucracy and perhaps specific producer interests, whereas the costs are spread out over the mass of consumers. The political support for nationalist economic policies is obtained on the basis of the gains they promise to their constituents, even if the total net benefits to all concerned tend to be negative.

As a policy, economic nationalism is encumbered by at least three biases.[3] First, it concentrates on industrialization and usually at the expense of agriculture. The objective here is to achieve a modern-looking nation-state as quickly as possible. The bias for industrialization is usually also very specific in terms of types of industries to encourage. The selection is more on the criteria of what leading developed nations possess than on comparative advantage and economic logic. The establishment of a steel industry, an automobile industry, and a national airline are but the more obvious cases in point.

The second bias is a preference for economic planning. There is the feeling that controls associated with planning enable a country to more quickly mobilize available resources to achieve other desired goals of nationalism. Imitation of the Soviet Union's experience and its rapid postrevolutionary development into a world power recommends a course of national economic planning to some people. There is, in general, the perception that the processes of economic development are speeded up as a result of planning. Finally, the elite and bureaucracy see in planning a direct means to exercise and enhance their power and prestige.

The third bias in a policy of economic nationalism is indiscriminate hostility to large multinational or transnational corporations. They are viewed as agents of colonialism and imperialism of the advanced countries in which they happen to have their headquarters and thus a threat to national sovereignty and independence. In effect, these corporations are viewed simply as an arm of the economic and political power of their parent countries. Since these corporations are more than likely independent entities they are viewed suspiciously both by host and parent countries. The parent countries complain that such corporations ought to invest and produce more at home than send employment opportunities abroad and create balance-of-payments problems for the country.

It may be that the nonpecuniary gains by the mass of the population from collective consumption aspects of nationalism offset the losses in primary income imposed on them by policies of economic nationalism, so that nationalistic policies do result in maximizing total satisfaction. It may also be that nationalistic policies are, in effect, the simplest and cheapest means to raise real income in some emerging countries.[4] Indeed, economic nationalism may so block economic growth it becomes necessary to resort to even more extreme nationalistic sentiment and policy as the only means available to maintain the illusion of economic development.

The economic significance of nationalism is thus to cultivate and extend property rights and jobs to nationals so as to satisfy their taste for nationalism. Confiscation and nationalization are ways for carrying out such a policy. This would include property and very likely jobs. Investment is another route whereby public funds are used to purchase property and create jobs and activities on behalf of nationals. It would also include imposing tariffs and in general protecting activities of nationals who would thereby receive higher prices that, in effect, are taxes imposed on the general consumer.

By reducing the efficiency of the country's economy, these by-products of economic nationalism will also reduce its real income. Disappointment with the economy's performance on this score increasingly pushes the government into the formation of prices and wages to assure desired outcomes. This will typically lead to price and wage controls. Since wage and price controls inevitably fail, the system is increasingly driven into collective participatory planning where wages and prices are determined. This may, in fact, be desired by some people. Nevertheless, such an arrangement offers little chance that the market system will be allowed to play its effective and efficient role.

The inevitable failure of price and wage controls is readily demonstrated by considering some problems and consequences of prices for individual products and services (including wages). The effects of a fixed price for a product or service depend in the first instance on the level at which it is fixed and whether it is a minimum or a maximum price.

To illustrate the issues, let us suppose we set up an administrative agency to fix prices. Now suppose this agency fixed the price of a commodity or service precisely at the level at which it would fall relative to other prices if there were no price controls and the price were established by free market forces. In this case, the price control will have no effect, and our agency will have performed a needless exercise. Of course, the administrative costs incurred by this exercise will be borne by the taxpayer.

Now suppose that our agency sets a fixed price that is a maximum price but that it sets the price at some level lower than what the price would be if it were determined by free market forces. In this case shortages will appear. People will want to buy more of the commodity or service than they otherwise would, but less of the product or service will be produced than otherwise would have been produced. Why should less of the product be produced at this lower price? The reason is simply that at this lower price it becomes more profitable to produce other items whose prices are not fixed at this lower level. Now if more is demanded than is supplied, then some system determines who among the people is going to get the product or service in question. This can be done by attaching another office to our price-administering agency, whose function will be to issue coupons, or the product or service can be given to old and regular customers of the suppliers, or it can be done according to the rule of "first come, first served." This is, of course, the familiar case of the queue with all the losses in time spent waiting one's turn.

If less of a product or service is produced because its price is fixed too low, it must be that fewer resources are employed. Now, what happened to those resources? They simply moved to other industries producing products and services whose prices were not controlled. Ironically, since prices that tend to be controlled in "essential" industries are not controlled in "unessential" industries, this means that price controls tend to cause fewer of the essential products or services to be produced and more of the unessential products or services.

The above need not be the case at all, some will say, since the government can induce producers of the commodity or service in question to produce more at this lower price by offering them an incentive in the form of a subsidy. All this means is that, in effect, producers now receive a higher price, raised "artificially" by the government subsidy. The taxpayer in general will now bear not only the cost of the price-administering agency but also the additional cost of the subsidy.

Consider our last case in which a minimum price is fixed at a level higher than that which would prevail in a free market. Now there will be initial surpluses. At the higher price for the product or service more will be produced. Instead of rationing consumers, it will not be necessary to "ration" the production of the product or service among the many producers who would be willing to produce at this higher price. Again, as in the case of consumers, this can be done by attaching an office to our price-administering agency whose function will be to allocate by quota production of the product or service in question.

This, in general, is the all-too-familiar problem in the past of U.S. agricultural surpluses. In this case, the taxpayer as a consumer will very likely pay the higher price for the product or service as well as the cost of the administering agency.

Selective price controls, moreover, cannot avoid discrimination. If a producer's selling price is fixed, there is usually an obligation to control his costs. This means fixing more than the prices of a producer's more obvious inputs such as labor and raw materials. It also means that such items as taxes, interest costs, and business costs must also be fixed.

Control of labor costs, however, is the most difficult. Such elements of labor costs as fringe benefits, compensation for overtime work, shift differentials, and paid leave serve to complicate the already difficult task of setting wage rates. The U.S. federal minimum wage example will suffice to illustrate the difficulties in setting wage rates.[5]

The inverse relation between changes in the minimum wage and substitution (capital for labor) effects one would expect from economic theory appears to be confirmed. When information on evasion and violations of the minimum wage law is taken into account, considerable light is shed on the complexities of wage fixing. In effect, an increase in the minimum wage is equivalent to a reduction in the price of evasion and avoidance. The price of evasion and avoidance is the cost of evasion and avoidance minus the benefits of evasion and avoidance. The benefit has increased with the increase in the minimum wage. And, other things being equal, one would expect evasion and avoidance of the minimum wage to increase. This also appears to be confirmed by the evidence.[6]

The minimum wage has had adverse effects on wage differentials,[7] and these differentials serve a useful purpose in allocating labor services into various occupations. They are, in fact, an essential part of the price mechanism. When they are subjected to an autonomous shock in the form of a government fiat, a compression of wage differentials occurs. The wages of those directly affected by the rise in the minimum wage rise more than wages of those not so directly affected. Since it is not as easy to allocate labor services as it is other services and goods, the problem of production adjustments is aggravated.

Matters are further complicated by difficulties in defining exactly what it is that is being controlled. Failure to specify accurately the end product or service leads to the inevitable tendency to increase profit margins by cutting quality, particularly where shortages already exist. The problem, moreover, is not simply one of quality deterioration. There is also the tendency for the variety of products to be reduced.

In the face of domestic price and wage ceilings, there is always the tendency for a producer to sell abroad at a higher price. When the producer is allocated fewer productive resources than he desires, he may seek to increase his supply by imports. This inevitably leads to price controls and physical controls over imports, such as foreign exchange controls and import and export quotas. The general direction into which a country adopting such controls is pushed forces its government and bureaucracy into a position as the sole judge on the volume and direction new investment will take. Government, and more specifically its bureaucracy, dominates the field of new investment through its policies regarding profits and sales.

Even more important, perhaps, failure to allow the market system to play its effective and efficient role almost assures that money and the monetary system will not be allowed to play a nondiscriminatory and autonomous role within the constraints of a rules-based policy system so necessary to assure the preservation of economic and monetary stability in the country.

Worse still, the pursuit of economic nationalism in today's interdependent world can be and indeed is a threat to worldwide stability. For small and emerging nations in particular it is a prescription for disaster since they are most likely to be dependent on foreign trade and the goodwill of other nations. Promoting economic nationalism through various protective measures invites and encourages retaliation by others. These activities serve to undermine the stability of not only the nation-state promoting economic nationalism but world stability and prosperity as well.

The sources, implications, and limitations of economic nationalism are examined in the following chapters against the economic and political history and experiences of several countries. Their experiences will be drawn upon to illustrate the issues at hand. These various strands are drawn together to gain insights into the problems and issues cast up by the pursuit of economic nationalism on the part of nation-states.

NOTES

1. See Harry G. Johnson, ed., *Economic Nationalism in Old and New States* (Chicago: University of Chicago Press, 1967); Albert Breton, "The Economics of

Nationalism," *Journal of Political Economy* 72 (1964): 376-86; Anthony Downs, *An Economic Theory of Democracy* (New York: Harper, 1957); Gary S. Becker, *The Economics of Discrimination* (Chicago: Univerity of Chicago Press, 1957); George Macesich, *Commercial Banking and Regional Development in the United States: 1950-60* (Tallahassee: Florida State University Press, 1963); George Macesich, *Yugoslavia: The Theory and Practice of Development Planning* (Charlottesville: University Press of Virginia, 1964); George Macesich, "The Theory of Economic Integration and the Experience of the Balkan and Danubian Countries Before 1914," *Proceedings of the First International Congress on Southeast European Studies*, Sofia, Bulgaria, 1966 and *Florida State University Slavic Papers I*, 1967; George Macesich, "Economic Theory and the Austro-Hungarian Ausgleich of 1867," in (Der osterreichisch-ungarische Ausgleich, 1867), edited by Ludovit Holitik (Bratislava: Slovak Academy, 1971); George Macesich, *Geldpolitik in einem gemeinsamen europaischen markt* (Money in a Common Market Setting) (Baden-Baden: Nomos Verlagsgellschaft, 1972); George Macesich, "Supply and Demand for Money in Canada," in *Varieties of Monetary Experience*, edited by David Meiselman (Chicago: University of Chicago Press, 1971), pp. 249-96.

2. See James M. Buchanan, *The Demand and Supply of Public Goods* (Chicago: Rand McNally, 1968); James Buchanan and Gordon Tullock, *The Calculus of Consent* (Ann Arbor: University of Michigan Press, 1962); Fred R. Gladbe and Dwight R. Lee, *Microeconomics: Theory and Applications* (New York: Harcourt Brace Jovanovich, 1980); Ronald Coase, "The Problem of Social Cost," *Journal of Law and Economics*, October 1960, pp. 1-45.

3. See Harry G. Johnson, "Ideology of Economic Policy in New States," in his *Economic Nationalism in Old and New States*, pp. 129-30.

4. See, for instance, Johnson, *Economic Nationalism in Old and New States*, p. 15.

5. See, for example, George Macesich and Charles T. Stewart, Jr., "Recent Department of Labor Studies of Minimum Wage Effects," *Southern Economic Journal*, April 1960; Marshall R. Colberg, "Minimum Wage Effects on Florida Economic Development," *Journal of Law and Economics*, October 1960; John M. Peterson, "Recent Needs in Minimum Wage Theory," *Southern Economic Journal*, July 1962; Yale Brozen, "Minimum Wages and Household Workers," *Journal of Law and Economics*, October 1962; and L. G. Reynolds, "Wages and Employment in the Labor-Surplus Economy," *American Economic Review*, March 1965.

6. Macesich and Stewart, "Recent Department of Labor Studies," p. 288ff.

7. George Macesich, "Are Wage Differentials Resilient? An Empirical Test," *Southern Economic Journal*, April 1961.

3

ECONOMIC NATIONALISM AND
EMERGING EUROPEAN NATION-STATES

THE EMERGING EUROPEAN NATION-STATE

This chapter examines the intellectual sources and economic implications of nationalism against the experience of emerging European nation-states. At the same time, some of the misunderstanding surrounding economic nationalism can be cleared by considering how it works in its historical perspective.[1] Though nationalism most often expresses itself in the political arena, deep underneath are motivating economic factors that give it content and direction. In this chapter we consider mercantilism when nationalism and economics were combined in a close nexus in European countries and their overseas dependencies from around 1500 to about 1800.

The body of loosely knit ideas and practices we now call mercantilism or economic nationalism developed and eclipsed gradually but not completely as testified in the legislative practices of modern nations. Mercantilism is the economic counterpart of political nationalism, and nationalism itself is a force in the development of nation-states. England, Spain, and France became nation-states rather early; Italy, Germany, and other Continental nation-states relatively late.

Most studies date English mercantilism from the end of the War of the Roses and the beginning of the reign of King Henry VII in 1485, though scattered evidence suggests a much earlier date. Mercantilism peaked in Queen Elizabeth's reign in the late 1500s and through the Stuart period in the 1600s. Much of the English mercantilist legislation was not removed from the books until the mid-nineteenth century, though many of the laws had not been enforced for years. In Spain mercantilism was in full bloom during the 1500s and 1600s. It peaked in France during the ministry of Colbert in the latter 1600s.

Historians sometimes say that revolutions occur when a social structure fails to adjust itself to conditions that call for change. In the revolt against feudalism and a cosmopolitan and unified Christendom, the growing forces of European social life created not only nation-states but also national churches, national cultures, and new theories and ideals. The political revolution, in effect, replaced the medieval ideal of a unified cosmopolitan clusteredom by the ideal of particularistic, independent, irresponsible, absolutely sovereign territorial states, the avowed santion of whose acts is power. A comparison of ideals leaves much to be desired on the part of nation-states. A comparison of realities, however, suggests that the nation-state, for all its shortcomings, is neither better nor worse than the private warfare of feudalism.

Indeed, we can argue that competitive nationalism provided the driving force for economic advance over the limited manorial and town economy of the Middle Ages. It provided, in a national economic unit, a greater division of labor and thus greater productivity and output as well as a richer and fuller intellectual life than anything hitherto possible. This redirection of energies marked the period of the "Commerical Revolution," which cast up political and economic conceptions as well as views on international relations that have not since changed appreciably.

This Commercial Revolution served, first, to concentrate energies on the national state rather than the town or manor, thereby increasing and deepening the scale of economic operations. Second, the very scale of operations served to limit society's cosmopolitan vision to the narrower particularistic nation-state. Third, these tendencies expressed in the Protestant revolt served to shift authority from the church to the civil government. By the close of the Middle Ages these changes transformed feudal loyalty to an individual lord into a broader and more comprehensive loyalty to country and countrymen.

For the first time there appeared in Europe what might definitely be called "national states," domains whose inhabitants were held together by a more or less vague but intensely real feeling of solidarity with their own kind and enmity to all others. It should be underscored that these nationalistic sentiments so common today are really not rooted in human nature per se, but appeared in a period of European history to serve a relatively small elite group of people, the so-called commercial middle class, so that they could obtain popular support for the political and social changes they advocated. Without such support it is very doubtful indeed that the small group of people who carried forth the Commercial Revolution would have been successful in a society still overwhelmingly agricultural.

The middle class joined its economic interest to the nationalist sentiments, of which it was the strongest and most vocal exponent, to push forward the movement for national sovereignty. It was an alliance common enough in history and in contemporary society, as this study argues, of one group both sharing and using for their own ends the powerful but fluid force of nationalism. These interests were first concentrated upon the king and monarchy and thus displaced the feudal landlords.

To be sure, other forces besides the interests of the middle class pushed forward the development of modern nationalism. The Hundred Years' War between England and France and the expulsion of the Moors from Spain and its subsequent union under one monarch both served to promote nationalism at the expense of the older localism of the Middle Ages. Internal factional strife, which exhausted and exterminated the competing baronial class, turned people toward the monarchy as a means for assuring peace and order and for promoting commerce and trade.

These developments under the Tudors had their effects in a rising tide of strong government in the interest of the middle classes and in the glorification of the monarchy as a symbol of a united and prosperous England. The expansion of English culture and literature during this period is well known. So too in France, following the expulsion of the English and the religious wars, the victory of the French patriots in the person of the first Bourbon, Henry IV, ushered in the creation of a great French literature in the seventeeth century.

It is this rise in national cultures that provided the principal ingredient in the formation of a nationalist sentiment. The growth of a large public interested in literature and learning, combined with the invention of the printing press, assured a vast audience capable of enjoying the luxury of books. Protestantism brought with it a translation of the Bible into the vernacular and served as a foundation for national literature encouraging schools and literacy. These influences served to eliminate the medieval difference between the languages of the various towns and to prevent differences in language from growing as a result of the rapidly changing spoken language, thus forcing the use of Latin as a common language for communication. They also had the effect of disrupting the Latin culture of Christendom, since it was possible to communicate in the vernacular language instead of Latin. Indeed those who persisted in the use of Latin as a communication vehicle found their influence continually diminished.

These turbulent years thus witnessed the emergence of a centralized national state, first through a series of struggles between the Papacy on the one hand and the feudal nobility on the other and the national monarch. Then the middle class, having used the monarch to break their other foes, aided by the Protestant sects, demanded and gained from him first fixed rights and then direct control, maintaining all the while the irresponsible sovereignty he had won.

Naturally, all of this called forth political theories and concepts to sustain the struggle. First, these had put forward the monarch against the divinely supported Papacy. Second, they had to set the monarch above the heritage of feudal custom and power. Third, theories and concepts had to be developed and/or made to serve to displace the monarch when his work was done and power was lodged in a national government so that the middle class could take over that power.

In sum, the power once held by the Papacy in the Middle Ages and in an age that did not recognize even in theory such concepts as irresponsible power and sovereignty (not to speak of a state of sovereign power) was transferred to the national state. The theory of omnipotence, which the pope held on the plea that any action might come under his cognizance if it concerned morality, had been taken over by the national state on the theory that any action, if it involved money or contract, must be a matter for the courts.

The political theorists who served to promote these changes rested their arguments on "rights and law" rather than on notions of utility and promotions of the general welfare. Those promoting change argued that it was their right, that they had some time-honored natural or divine law on their side. Those resisting such changes insisted in opposition that theirs was the "right and law."

The net effect was that a strong centralized state capable of preserving law and order and encouraging trade and commerce rested on two theories. One theory, the divine right of kings, aimed at the claim of the pope to be the sole divine source of power. The other, which dealt with the theory of the absolute sovereignty of the territorial monarch, was aimed at the barons. The divine right of kings emancipated the civil government from the pope and the clergy and their claims on temporal matters. Accordingly, the secular government was as divinely ordained as the ecclesiastical and thus free to order its own affairs. In the subsequent struggles the divine right of kings ultimately coalesced with the right of national sovereignty and independence.

It was, however, left to Machiavelli in Italy, Bodin in France, and Hobbes in England to develop concepts in support of the divine right of kings or despotism that were later of use in combating it. They also firmly established the sovereignty of the national state on rational rather than religious grounds. Hobbes's contribution is particularly significant for later developments for he based his theory upon the same popular basis as the Protestant contenders.

It is, however, the social contract with antecedents in Roman law that is singularly important for political thought. The theory holds that all civil authority resting originally in the people has been conferred by them upon the ruler in order that he may perform certain necessary functions. As such it may be used to assert the supreme authority of the ruler as being endowed with all authority or the fundamental authority of the people as the ultimate source of that authority. The first interpretation was used by the princes against the church, the second by the opponents of civil despotism in the churches and the middle class. Hobbes used it to establish a strong despotic state. Peace and defense are the end of the contract; obedience to the sovereign must be rendered until he proves impotent to enforce them, when the contract is dissolved and a new one made. It was thus no problem for Hobbes to support either Charles I or Cromwell. It makes no difference who the sovereign is, only that he be powerful.

Rationalized by John Locke, the contract theory became the starting point of political thought in the eighteenth century. It was made the foundation of the Dutch and British governments. In fact, most antimonarchists derived sovereign power from the people by some form of the social contract, and held the king responsible to them for his deeds.

It was in commercial Holland that we had for the first time the ideal of a constitutional monarch governing for the sake of securing the people's spiritual welfare and material prosperity. It was in fact the very type achieved by England in 1689 and rationalized by John Locke and justified in popular sovereignty—the social contract and natural rights. These were the beginnings of the concept of federalism destined to be so important to the United States and other countries.

MERCANTILIST IDEAS AND POLICIES

Our discussion thus far has focused on the emerging European national state as the instrument for the aggrandizement of the commercial middle class at the expense of nobles and clergy. The middle class, supported by nationalistic sentiment and the desire of religious bodies to maintain their existence, created the absolutistic national state out of the medieval hierarchical order and then limited that state when it sought to attack property and conscience. Once established, these new governments were vehicles for the regulation of economic affairs. As in political affairs, the movement was away from the small unit such as the manor, town, and guild toward regulation on a national level. These smaller units were incorporated into the national effort and directed toward increasing the prosperity of the country and particularly its commercial middle class.

These changes in the regulating unit and its purpose encapsulate the collection of economic ideas known as "mercantilism," which might be better called "economic nationalism." It is the conscious purpose of employing government regulation to build up a great power and the building up of such a power to increase the gains of the commercial middle class.

Thomas Mun's *England's Treasure by Foreign Trade*, published in 1664, remains one of the economic classics on the subject of mercantilism. It is, according to Mun, nation against nation. A country must have a favorable balance of trade. It must sell more abroad yearly than it imports. The difference between exports and imports will be brought home in the form of specie, that is, gold and silver. Foreign trade is the road to national wealth. Domestic trade, on the other hand, means that a gain to one domestic party is but a loss to another domestic party. In foreign trade it does not matter since the other party is a foreigner. In effect, mercantilism incorporates the medieval idea that trade per se can never produce new value.

Money, according to Mun, encourages trade, which in turn increases money, and which will enlarge the state treasury and provide the sinews of war and peace alike, and thus it is the first requisite of a strong national government. To this end, export of raw materials was prohibited and bounties for the export of manufactures established. The accumulation of "national wealth" was promoted as the aim that would justify every expedient, and the whole power of the nation was turned toward developing the profits of favored merchants. One industry was fostered, another discouraged, charters were granted and monopolies established, colonies were estates to be exploited for the benefit of the home merchants, and the world was parceled out among privileged companies, which watched over the lives and fortunes of their patriotic and prosperous members.

The nation-state also took upon itself the difficult task of the supervision over the methods and quality of goods that was formerly carried out by the guilds. The net result was that outmoded production methods were perpetuated and improvement prevented. The new nation-centralized state simply proved itself incompetent to supervise the details of the country's output of goods and services. The problems so created have their contemporary dimensions in current planning and regulating efforts on the part of modern nation-states.

Thus, in the bundle of ideas called "mercantilism" two propositions are prominent. One is that the wealth of a country consists of the quantity of gold and silver in circulation. The second is that the way to increase that wealth is to secure a surplus in the balance of payments typically identified with the balance of trade, by policies of import substitution and export promotion.

Whether or not mercantilist writers really wrote and thought that money was wealth can best be judged by turning to their writings. We have noted Mun's contributions. There are others.

John Hales, who died in 1571, in a study usually attributed to him, *Discourse of the Common Ward of This Realm of England* (1581), drew on a mixture of old medieval and new commercial ideas in his discussion on the nature of goods contained in England's foreign trade.[2] Some goods were useful, for example, gold, silver, wool, and skins, while others were not, for example, girdles, and so on. Trade in useful goods should be encouraged and in useless goods discouraged. There is even to be found in the *Discourse* an acceptance of what subsequently became known as the quantity theory of money—the idea that the price level depends on the quantity of money.

There is, moreover, in the *Discourse* an examination of how the different classes within a country are affected by price inflation. Those on fixed incomes were hurt while those benefiting from an upward movement in price were helped. The former included landowners whose rents were fixed, laborers, artisans, and indeed the king as well. The merchants and others who were able to increase the prices of their goods and services were helped by price inflation.

Specie should be used, according to the *Discourse*, to repay debt according to its specie value at the time the debt was incurred. Specie was also useful to the nation in terms of the war chest it provided as well as to pay for purchases of grain from abroad if there was a crop failure. This latter point appears repeatedly in mercantilist writings.

Jean Bodin (1530-96) was a French lawyer whose work, *The Six Books of the Republic* (Les six livres de la République), (1576), is considered a classic on political thought. In an earlier study on prices (1568), Bodin argued that price rises can be attributed more to the influx of gold and silver from South America than to the depreciation of the metal content of coins as asserted by some people, including the controller of the French mint. Drawing on a mercantilist argument he also asserted that a favorable balance of trade that brought in specie was to be encouraged.

Barthilem de Laffemos (ca.1545-1611) considered gold and silver as a measure of wealth. In a number of published works he argued that the quantity of gold and silver in a country can better be increased by developing its industries than by preventing the export of precious metals. In his view, government should encourage and expand domestic industry, establish workshops to employ the idle, and prohibit the export of raw materials. Many of Laffemos's proposals were later adopted by Colbert.

Antoine de Montchretien (ca.1571-1621), another French writer whose study, *Treatise on Political Economy* (Traité de l'économie politique) (1615), appears the first to be so titled, argues that national wealth is the product of a country's industry and not simply its hoard of specie. Government should actively promote industry and its development. Trade is to be regulated and duties placed on the export of raw materials. The importation of manufactured products, in his view, is to be prohibited.

In Austria, Philipp Wilhelm von Hornich (1638-1713), in a study, *Austria Over All, If Only She Will* (Oesterreich über alles, wann es nur will) (1684), proposed a program for the economic revival of the Austrian Empire. His program called for a full exploration of the country's resources. Domestic manufacturing should be encouraged over the importation of such products. Austrians should be trained in the industrial arts and trades with instructors brought in from abroad if necessary. Specie should be kept in domestic circulation and neither hoarded nor exported. The country should abstain from consuming imported goods, especially luxuries. If such goods were to be imported they should be bought directly from those producing such goods and paid for by Austrian goods and not specie. Foreign markets should be sought out for the country's surplus goods. Inputs should be prohibited when domestic goods are available, regardless of political alliances and friendships.

Sir Josiah Child (1630-99), in his study, *Brief Observations Concerning Trade and the Interest of Money* (1668) and later expanded and republished in 1693, argues for a favorable balance of trade. More important, he discusses the relationship between the rate of interest and the state of trade later associated with Wicksell. Child compares England, which had a high interest rate, to Holland, which had a low one, arguing that a trading project that was profitable in Holland would be unprofitable in England because of the difference in interest rates.

It was William Patterson (1658-1719), whose plan for a note-issuing bank, led to the establishment of the Bank of England in 1694. It was an idea expressed earlier by William Potter that called for the issue of bills drawn on the security of land and other property.

A similar plan was carried out in France by John Law (1671-1729). In his study, *Money and Trade Consider'd; With a Proposal for Supplying the Nation With Money* (1705, 2d edition, 1720), he argued that trade depends on money and that laws designed to accord employment have little success if money is scarce. He argued for issuing more money for the purpose of encouraging trade. On the basis of his idea the French government established a note-issuing bank. And indeed a boom was created only to be followed by inflation and repudiation of Law's idea. More successful, however, was Patterson's plan for the Bank of England, which called for a limited issue of notes backed by government securities with gold backing for all notes over the given limit.

In Germany during the eighteenth century a movement with significant mercantilist elements called "Cameralist"—or Cameralwissenschaft, the science of government counting house, as distinct from Polizeiwissenschaft, the science of "police" or government administration—gained a considerable following. The movement included such writers as Johannes Heinrich Gottlieb von Justi (1717-71) and Joachim Georg Darjes (1714-91). Darjes's writings included *First Principles of Cameralism* (Erst Gründe der Cameralwissenschaften) (1756) and *Principles of Government Administration* (Grundsätze der Polizeiwissenschaft) (1756); and Justi wrote *System of Finances* (System des Finanzwesens) (1766).

Though they focused mainly on government revenue and finance, Cameralist writers also put forward some general principles applicable to national development. They argued, essentially, that in the management of a state, just as in the management of a household, the ultimate purposes are to acquire the means to assure what has been acquired and to use reasonably the goods possessed. In state management, housekeeping is considerably more extensive than in the private household.

Justi pushed forward a set of principles on taxation that Adam Smith later incorporated into *The Wealth of Nations* as canons or rules of taxation. Briefly, Justi argued that taxes should be such as to be paid willingly. Such taxes should not be oppressive to industry and trade nor should they limit the freedom of the people. The taxes should be levied fairly or equally. They should be levied on definite objects and not in such a manner as to be easily evaded. Their costs of collection should not be high. They should be payable at a convenient time and in an acceptable manner.

The Cameralists incorporated typical mercantilist elements into their program as well. Foreign trade was to be encouraged so long as it brought in more specie than flowed out of the country. Importation of luxuries and the export of specie were discouraged. Capable, competent, and rich foreigners were encouraged to settle in the country.

A characteristic of mercantilist policies that distinguished them from the earlier medieval policies is that they tended to tax imports and provide subsidies to exports. Earlier the tendency was to tax both imports and exports. Mercantilist policies, in effect, turned from goods to money, to the increase in the stock of money, and to encouragement of exports and discouragement of imports. In this manner the producer was helped at the expense of the consumer. To be sure, even at the height of mercantilism, the interests of the producers were not always dominant. Thus the English corn laws had the consumer in mind as well as the producer. As indeed did the "Statute of Monopolies," which was designed to protect the consumer from the more obvious damages brought about by modern interests.

Many laws designed to protect the producer also have domestic employment as their goal. Domestic employment and development of home industry was the stated goal of duties imposed, for instance, by the French and Swedish governments in the mid-1600s against English cloth.

The emigration of artisans was of considerable concern to nation-states. Laws discouraging such movement were on the books of most countries during the mercantilist period. Indeed, in 1719 the British government prohibited the emigration of skilled workers, though the law itself was evaded. Patents and monopolies were extended to foreigners to entice them to settle and develop new industries. Machinery, on the other hand, was not to be exported nor indeed were drawings of such machinery.

Seapower played an important role in the mercantilist scheme of things, so shipping and ships were very important. Exports were to be carried in domestic ships. Explorations and colonies were encouraged and trading opportunities cultivated. The objective was to make the home country a focus of empire with the wealth and power that such a position commanded.

In England laws encouraged colonial as well as British shipping. Indeed it was not until the middle of the nineteenth century that British navigation laws were repealed. Along with the policy of protecting domestic manufacturers, those in the colonies were repressed. The reaction to such action in the colonies generated protests and other disturbances, including open revolution in the British American colonies that subsequently became the United States.

In France during the ministry of Jean Baptiste Colbert (1619-83) mercantilist policy reached a peak. Government service was reformed and improved. Industry was regulated in considerable detail. Companies were established to trade with America and India. Restrictions were imposed on the emigration of artisans and craftsmen. The merchant marine and navy were expanded and strengthened.

Spain, whose explorers and soldiers in South America sent to the home country vast quantities of precious metals, was viewed with envy and fear by the other growing nation-states. Indeed the growing economic and naval power of Spain prompted England to undertake like measures in self-defense. Spain was later displaced in English eyes as a threat by Holland and France in the 1600s and 1700s.

Policies in Spain were decidedly of mercantilist flavor. Laws forbade exports in foreign ships when Spanish ships were available. In fact, sea trade was very closely controlled in good measure for defense purposes. Domestic industry was protected. Gold and silver were not to be exported, even though Spanish trade was in fact distributing the precious metals throughout Europe.

In sum, mercantilist policies focused on building national strength, even at the expense of individual welfare and wealth. The state and not necessarily the individual formed the foundations upon which policies and laws were based. Wealth in their view was not maximized by free private individual enterprise. Indeed, mercantilist policies did not view as correct the maximization of individual wealth within the nation and through it the achievement of national wealth as Adam Smith argues in *The Wealth of Nations*. Mercantilist policies can better be interpreted as placing on a national basis the medieval policies that focused on regulations whose aim was to achieve a balance among various classes of people with a modicum of justice for all.

The principles and policies of mercantilism have been repeatedly challenged. They have, nonetheless, never been completely repudiated in the legislative halls of nation-states. On the contrary, these principles and policies maintain a remarkable vitality as this study indicates.

Nevertheless, the seeds of individual liberty were at work even in the mercantilist world. The emerging middle class ceased to support absolutism when it ceased to serve its commercial interests, particularly in such matters as property rights. Even Machiavelli and Bodin counseled against the taking of private property by the sovereign without just cause. It was precisely at this point that absolute monarchy broke down. It simply was not wise enough to incorporate such advice into its program of action when dealing with the rights of property.

The issue of property rights coalesced with religious freedom and popular rights, the middle class making up the bulk of support for such rights. The assault upon the absolute monarchy, prompted by religious groups demanding toleration, quickly gathered in support others to whom the freedom of conscience appealed and ultimately their participation in the defense of property rights. To be sure, the toleration of these groups when in power for the rights of others leaves much to be desired. When their own rights are threatened, however, they are very strenuous indeed in their defense. Most of the arguments come from the dissenting Protestant groups, but when Catholics sensed their own rights in jeopardy they waxed eloquent against despotism. Indeed, two of the greatest defenses of popular sovereignty were written by the Spanish Jesuits Mariana and Suarez.

It was Machiavelli's principles, however, that rising national states adopted almost to the letter. These called for freedom from all superior codes or laws whatsoever. In these precepts Machiavelli followed the example of the Papacy, which was sovereign as no other state. Though theoretically bound by natural law, the pope could dispense with violations of it. Faith need not be kept with heretics as the Council of Constance had decreed in its dealings with John Hus. Machiavelli read "state" for "church" and "enemy" for "heretic" and founded the modern religion of the state.

It was left to Grotius in his *Rights of War and Peace* (1625) to provide some constraints to the unbridled exercise of national sovereignty. His study provides a semblance of a code of honor and/or rules of the game and thus some constraints on the ceaseless struggle among sovereign nations. Drawing on Roman *jus gentium*, or law of nations and natural law, Grotius attempts to place before nations the idea that they do constitute a society and are obligated not to violate too outrageously established custom.

Nations may wage war in accordance with natural law. They must never forget, however, that even among enemies there is a common bond of humanity. If war is carried out it should be done so as to make peace possible. With the dissolution of the old society of Christendom under the sovereignty of the pope and canon law, the new sovereign states did search out, however reluctantly, for a new social contract and some binding law over them. The international law so derived does provide for something in common among nation-states and serves to constrain their actions, if not always successfully.

It is not difficult to understand the appeal of natural law and natural rights for a people whose traditional moorings had been broken by mercantilist policies. They provided something more permanent than the human view of what is correct, fair, and just. Natural law provided permanence and binding power. Greeks and Romans earlier had provided for such power. Indeed, in Stoicism nature is a great rational process; the soul of order and right was spread to all the Roman rulers. Since Roman *jus civilis* applied only to Roman citizens, Roman jurists developed *jus gentium*, a law of the people of all nations that was interlaced with the Stoic ideal of a law of nature.

In effect, the law of nature and the law of nations were synthesized into a law that natural reason had established among men. The reintroduction of Roman law in the twelfth century—the concept of a system of rights and justice independent of the human element—was seized upon as the most effective vehicle for criticizing all institutions, whether papal, monarchy, or other institutional arrangements.

With the development of the physical sciences and the discovery of harmonious and immutable laws of nature, a powerful support for the legal and moral principle of natural law was provided. Nature provided not only the foundation for the physical and mathematical laws, but for the moral and legal laws as well. Natural law became the basis of natural rights and universal obligations. It thus lent itself to the purpose of restraining the internal and external affairs of sovereign nations. It also served to undermine many of the mercantilist policies put into place by the absolute monarchies of national states as we shall discuss next in our survey of the thoughts of economists toward government intervention into economic affairs.

NOTES

1. For a useful discussion of mercantilism and the rise of trade and commerce, see, for instance, Dudley Dillard, *Economic Development of the North Atlantic Community* (Englewood Cliffs, N.J.: Prentice Hall, 1962); Max Weber, *The Protestant Ethic and the Spirit of Capitalism* (New York: Scribners, 1958); Richard H. Tawney, *Religion and the Rise of Capitalism* (New York: Mentor Books, 1954); Edgar S. Furniss, *The Position of the Laborer in a System of Nationalism* (New York: Augustus M. Kelley, 1965); J. Viner, *Studies in the Theory of International Trade* (New York: Harper & Brothers, 1937); E. Troelsch, *The Social Teaching of the Christian Churches*, trans. O. Wyon, 2 Vols. (New York: Macmillan, 1931); R. Schlatter, *Private Property: The History of an Idea* (New Brunswick, N.J.: Rutgers University Press, 1951); E. Lipson, *The Economic History of England*, 3 Vols. (New York: Macmillan, 1915-31); E. F. Hecksher, *Mercantilism*, trans. M. Shapiro, 2 Vols. (New York: Macmillan, 1935); H. Higgs, *The Physiocrats* (New York: Macmillan, 1897); W. J. Ashley, *An Introduction to English Economic History and Theory*, 2 Vols. (London: Longman, Green, 1888-93); M. Beer, *Early British Economics* (New York: Macmillan, 1938); A. J. and R. W. Carlyle, *A History of Medieval Political Theory in the West*, 6 Vols. (Edinburgh and London: William Blackwood, 1890); C. W. Cole, *Colbert and a Century of French Mercantilism* (New York: Columbia University Press, 1939); J. W. Angell, *The Theory of International Prices* (Cambridge, Mass.: Harvard University Press, 1926).

2. See Edmund Whittaker, *Schools and Streams of Economic Thought* (Chicago: Rand McNally, 1961), pp. 35-38.

4

COSMOPOLITANISM
AND ITS DETRACTORS: THE CLASSICAL AND
CONTINENTAL SCHOOLS

ADAM SMITH AND THE CLASSICAL SCHOOL

An immediate reason for Adam Smith's *The Wealth of Nations* (1776) is to combat mercantilism or economic nationalism. Unlike the mercantilists, Adam Smith and his followers in the classical school argued that wealth was maximized by the enterprise and self-interest of individuals and that restraints on trade in effect defeated the end they aimed at and discouraged the very employment and wealth they sought to promote. Maximization of individual wealth within the nation would result in greater national wealth. This is in fact a recurrent issue in economic policy between the individualism and cosmopolitanism of classical economics and the particularlism underpinning mercantilism or economic nationalism of a nation-state.[1] This chapter discusses the ideas underlying the cosmopolitanism of the classical school and that of the more nationalistic continental European schools.

The moral dilemma between individual and social benefits with which social philosophers and moralists wrestled is resolved by Adam Smith in his analysis of the market economy. His system of natural liberty, free markets, free men, and competition led to an orderly increase in the wealth of the nation. The free competitive play of individual selfishness was shown by Smith to be the source of economic growth, social order, and general welfare. Individualism did not lead to chaos but to order and prosperity.

Smith did more. He provided economics with an analytical framework. The idea was of a competitive self-adjusting market equilibrium following a path of growth and affluence. At the same time, *The Wealth of Nations* is a philosophical treatise concerned with fundamental problems of order and chaos in human society. Smith provided what came to be, especially in England and the United States, the orthodox approach to economic problems and policy that is very much alive in the twentieth century.

Critics seize upon two limitations to Smith's analysis of the free market. One is the distribution of income, which if highly unequal will signal the market to provide more for the rich and little for the poor. If the distribution of income is wrong, so too will production be wrong, however efficiently the market works to produce the goods and services. It is this very problem, in fact, that the early socialists raised and that Karl Marx (1818-83) later developed into a theory for the breakdown of capitalism.

The second criticism, closely related to the issue of economic justice, concerns private property in land and capital. Smith's support for the institution of private property as both natural and necessary to the preservation of economic incentives is good liberal doctrine. The fact is, however, that he supports it only in advanced societies. In primitive societies, only labor is considered a factor of production and thus rewarded by wages. Conversely, in advanced societies rent on land and profit on capital are also part of the costs of production. Since rent and profit as costs of production are really the products of social organization, and not natural phenomena like human labor and the motive of self-interest, Smith's idea of an equilibrium of natural forces in the market is compromised.

These shortfalls provide socialists, among others, an opening to argue that only a return to labor is natural. Accordingly, only when the full value of output is gained by labor through social ownership of the means of production (land and capital) would the natural state of society be regained. Economic justice would be served since the entire product of society would go to its producers, and society's demand would not be distorted by unearned income.

Thomas R. Malthus (1766-1834), David Ricardo (1772-1823), Jeremy Bentham (1748-1832), and Jean Baptiste Say (1767-1832) contributed enormously to the body of ideas now called Classical Economics. Writing at the close of the eighteenth century and during the turbulent early years of the nineteenth century, they promoted economics to a "science." These were the years of political, social, and technological revolutions that wiped away the vestiges of feudalism and the old aristocratic order. Much was expected of the American and French revolutions by English intellectuals and others. Some attribute the success of the American revolutionaries to the support of English liberals. Political reform in England was at the time a pressing issue. Even the French Revolution was looked upon favorably because it would bring democracy to France and thus peace to both countries.

The disappointment was all the greater when the wars with France began and continued for almost two decades. The Napoleonic period dashed all hopes for liberal political reforms in England. The Establishment concerned itself with holding the line and rooting out the "radicals." Cases in point are: the suspension in 1795 of the Habeas Corpus Act for five years; in 1799 the Anti-Combination Laws, prohibiting any combination of workers or employers for the purpose of regulating conditions of employment (for the most part these laws were directed and enforced more against labor than management). Suppression ruled these turbulent years.

Nevertheless, problems created by rapid change brought about by the war years demanded attention. The most obvious concerned the poor displaced by the economic, political, and social turmoil of the period. Their numbers increased as a result of demobilization following the Napoleonic wars. Enclosures of common land, displacing many farmers from their small plots, served to promote the growth of cities already overburdened with problems of poverty. Reaction against the French Revolution assured that the problems of the poor would receive little priority from conservative policymakers, particularly if solutions required political and social reforms. Still, something had to be done.

A solution of a sort was given by a religious minister, Thomas Robert Malthus. It is a solution consistent with the preservation of the status quo and one calling for minimal government intervention. Government, argued Malthus, can do little in any case since the problem of the poor is moral. The problem has its origins in two propositions. One is in the food supply; the other is in the sexual proclivities of man. The result is Malthus's principle that "the power of population is infinitely greater than the power in the earth to produce subsistence for man."

In effect, "misery and vice" hold population in check. If the supply of food increases, there is a corresponding increase in population until it is brought back to subsistence level, at which point population increase will stop. Wages tend toward the subsistence level, which is the *natural* wage. Any increase in wages above the natural or subsistence level causes the population to grow and subsequently for wages to decline. If, on the other hand, the price of food increases, wages would be forced up to maintain the subsistence wage. Moreover, increasing relief to the poor would mean taking resources out of the hands of those willing to invest, thus increasing output.

The implications for the poor are ominous. Relief payment simply raises the wages of the poor above subsistence and so results in more people. No increase in food production takes place as poverty continues unabated. Not a very happy state of affairs, but one for which the government and the conservative establishment are not to blame. Nature must be allowed to take its course.

For David Ricardo, capital accumulation is the mainspring of growth. Economic policy is to be directed to facilitating and promoting such accumulations. His model is based on the belief that economic freedom leads to maximum profits, which are the source of investment capital, and in a competitive economy leads to profit-maximum economic growth.

The political and social issues in England following the Napoleonic wars turned in part on whether the country should become more heavily industrialized or preserve a balance with agriculture. The issues involved, among others, the role of England's landed aristocracy in the country's social and political system. The contest was drawn in Parliament on the so-called Corn Laws and the import of grain into England. Existing laws protected English agriculture against foreign competition without at the same time resulting in "significant" price increases for food. They were, in effect, remnants of earlier mercantilist policies.

As a result of war-created increases in demand for agricultural products, English farmers and landed interests pushed for the enforcement of the Corn Laws as a means for preserving their prosperity. All sorts of schemes were put forward for promoting agriculture as England's leading industry.

All this was anathema to the British business community, which saw high food prices and high wages, reduced profits, and decreased exports spelling general ruin for British industry. They demanded nothing less than repeal of the Corn Laws. Ricardo and other economists entered the debate on the side of business interests and against those of agriculture. Ricardo, in effect, argued that it is the landowners and not farmers as such who benefit if the price of wheat is raised by tariffs. The high price of wheat enables an extension in the amount of land under cultivation that would not normally be profitable. The result is that in the older wheat-growing areas, landowners would raise rents to take advantage of the higher prices received by farmers. Consequently, a larger proportion of the nation's income would go to land-owners, who would use these additional resources not for productive investment but rather for "luxury expenditures."

Moreover, additional capital and labor would be drawn from industry to enlarged agricultural production stimulated by artificially high food prices. The net result would be to distort the nation's productive pattern, retarding the country's *natural* development of industry. Ricardo noted that high food prices would require high wages and thus high costs of production in industry. Since England must sell the products of industry throughout the world, higher costs would reduce business for English exports and so reduce the level of output of industry. Profits would be reduced, thereby slowing capital accumulation and economic growth, owing to both a lack of incentive and resources out of which to invest.

If left alone, a country's economy will achieve the maximum growth possible, according to Ricardo. It is, therefore, important that business be left alone to pursue profits, thus would the nation maximize the amount of saving and capital accumulation so necessary for growth. Government intervention would simply make the process of saving and accumulation all the more difficult. Ricardo, in effect, reinforced the theoretical and ideological underpinnings set in place by Adam Smith. Business interests are indeed well served by Ricardo's analysis.

The facility with which the international economy is integrated into Ricardo's model served to reduce all economic phenomena to fundamental relationships among factors of production. It demonstrates that the international division and specialization of labor is advantageous to all nations and that protection of domestic producers serves simply to damage the country imposing such protection. Free trade is beneficial internationally as well as domestically. The famous law of comparative advantage is used in support of the free trade doctrine. Moreover, capital will seek out countries where the returns are highest, provided such nations assure political stability and offer protection for private property rights. All of this remains very much part of contemporary international trade theory, if not practice.

The realization of the full benefits of free international trade made necessary a sound international monetary and financial system. We shall have more to say on Ricardo's views on the issue later. Suffice it here to note that he insisted that the domestic monetary system should be regulated so as to minimize any disruption in the international division of labor. Ricardo adopted a "bullionist" position, arguing that the domestic money supply should be directly tied to the country's gold supply. Such an arrangement assures that a country suffering a loss of gold through an unfavorable balance of trade automatically contracts its paper note issue. Contraction in the money supply thus tends to depress the country's general level of prices, which in turn encourages the desired adjustment in international accounts. The deficit country's exports become more attractive to foreigners while imports compete less successfully in home markets as the price of home-produced items decline. Ricardo, in effect, set out in its essentials the classical theory of the gold standard.

The monetary idea that money used as a standard of value consists of bank notes redeemable in specie or bullion and that coins circulate at their value as bullion is central to the body of classical ideas. This money is assumed to be convertible into gold or silver bars and to be freely exchangeable either as coin or as bullion between countries. Its value is fixed at its bullion value, and the rate of exchange between two currencies is easily calculated by comparing the intrinsic value of the precious metals that would automatically adjust to the "needs of trade" in each country.

Moreover, there is nothing that governments can do about this. If they issued paper money beyond the amount that the public would accept in the belief that these notes could at any moment be converted into gold, the surplus issue would be cashed and the government would have to redeem it with gold and silver from its reserves. If the notes are made inconvertible, their value would fall and the price of gold— indeed of all commodities—as measured in the paper money would rise in proportion to their overissue. This is Ricardo's argument published in his pamphlet (1810) entitled *The High Rise of Bullion: A Proof of the Depreciation of Bank Notes.*

The conclusion drawn by classical theorists is that governments must accept the fact that only true money (gold and silver, or specie) is beyond their control. All the elaborate government devices for increasing national supplies of specie are self-defeating. Money accommodates itself to the "needs of trade." If governments issue inferior monetary substitutes, their value will depreciate. There is no place, therefore, in the classical theory for discretionary interventionist monetary policies designed to maintain full employment, balance-of-payments equilibrium, or to combat inflation or depression.

It remained to be demonstrated that a free market would also achieve full employment of all resources, including labor and capital. That this in fact appears to be the case is demonstrated by Jean Baptiste Say (1767-1832) in his *Treatise on Political Economy*, which first appeared in 1803. The principle is Say's Law of Markets. According to Say, there can never be a general deficiency of demand or a glut of commodities throughout the economy. While there may be given sectors or industries in which overproduction may occur, along with a shortage in others, this is only a temporary situation. The fall in prices in one area and their rise in other areas will provide incentives for businessmen to shift production and thereby correct the situation.

Say pointed out that people produce in order to exchange their products for other products. Production thus creates its own demand. It is therefore impossible for production in general to outrun demand. Say's Law of Markets dominated economic thought on the level of economic activity until the concept was challenged by John Maynard Keynes in the 1930s.

Jeremy Bentham (1748-1832) and such "philosophical radicals" as James Mill, David Ricardo, and John Stuart Mill agitated for political reform, democratic government, and majority rule. The utilitarian political philosophy that dominated the "radicals" called for nothing less than a social system based upon full democratic participation and majority rule. According to Bentham and his utilitarian followers, this is the only way that a social system can maximize its total welfare and distribute it as widely as possible.

Bentham differs significantly from the classical liberalism of the eighteenth century, which emphasizes individual freedom as the end goal of public policy. He sees potential conflict in the idea that only individual action can create welfare. It is possible, for instance, that the action of one person in pursuit of his own interest may injure another and so reduce his welfare. After all, argues Bentham, human society is organized by man-made institutional arrangements. Conscious action can create social forms that enable men to live better. In effect, classical liberalism establishes by way of Benthamite utilitarianism a place for interventionist liberalism emphasizing social welfare. It is intervention and reform justified in terms of individual and social welfare and the "greatest good for the greatest number."

Thanks to Benthamite ideas, economics could henceforth easily incorporate the most laissez-faire individualist as well as the most thoroughgoing social reformer. The analytical apparatus is the same for both. The important differences arise from the assumptions and conclusions that each reach. This is an attribute that economists preserve to the present time.

All was not well in the post-Napoleonic world. The French Revolution did not bring forth "liberty, equality, and fraternity," nor did the rapid economic and technological advance usually called the "Industrial Revolution" abolish poverty. Indeed, the post-Napoleonic reaction and repression and the reestablishment of old political, social, and economic privileges served to increase poverty and arrest democratic advances for the general public. Critics seize upon the observed inequalities to push from theory to practice an alternative vision of society. It is a vision based on the cooperative element in man's nature, rather than the materialistic profit motive of private capitalism, and egalitarianism in place of the unequal distribution of income that prevailed at that time. To these early socialist critics, society is an organic whole composed of classes, rather than independent individuals as held by classical economists. The roots of modern socialism are in the post-Napoleonic Europe nurtured by reaction against economic and political circumstances of the era.

Private property and private ownership of the means of production, argue the socialists, is the root cause of the failure of the two great revolutions to abolish poverty and create a political order of full democracy. A few owners of capital benefited from these social and technological revolutions while the majority of people remained mired in poverty. The socialists called for the abolishment of private property and privilege as a first step into a new society of greater opportunity and dignity for all people.

The humanitarian and idealistic roots of early socialism is typified in the work and writing of Robert Owen (1771-1858). His attempts to establish, in England and the United States, cooperative communities in which land was owned in common and worker-owned enterprises in which profit was not permitted were not particularly successful. This is not surprising, since individualism dominated the era.

Unlike the utopian reformers, Karl Marx (1818-83) coupled scholarship with revolutionary agitation. It is not enough, according to Marx, to theorize; one must build a revolutionary party capable of seizing power when capitalism collapses. He did not suffer lightly other socialists who happened to disagree with his views. In fact, he established the practice of the vitriolic denunciation of opposing views that burdens so much contemporary socialist literature.

In Marx's view, capitalism (a term he invented) is doomed. His demonstration of its demise draws on so-called laws of motion of capitalist society. On one level Marx bases his argument on the inherent injustices of capitalism that lead ultimately to economic and social conditions that cannot be maintained. At another level his argument is sociological in that class conflict between increasingly affluent capitalists and an increasingly miserable working class will break out in social revolution. At still another level the argument is economic in that the accumulation of capital in private hands, while creating increasing abundance, also leads to the inevitable breakdown of capitalism. At all three levels the idea of conflict is underscored: conflict between ideal and reality—the moral issue; conflict between labor and capital—the sociological issue; conflict between growth and stagnation—the economic issue. This conflict generates change, and so capitalism, according to Marx, must eventually give way to another social system in which conflict is replaced by ethical, social, and economic harmony. This change is the "dialectical process" whereby socialism will replace capitalism. Thus Marx created one of the world's most powerful ideologies whose vision of abundance, equality, and freedom stands in challenge to classical-liberal individualism, private property, and private enterprise.

THE CONTINENTAL EUROPEAN SCHOOL

The fact of the matter is that Great Britain, in which the classical school of economics emerged and grew, was much more advanced than the continents of Europe and America. Thanks in part to its geography, which afforded it a measure of security, Britain, unlike other countries in Europe, was able to develop a modern industrial base relatively early. Earlier mercantilist policies undoubtedly also helped to channel resources to prepare the foundation for Britain's industrial advance. And when to this is added the available human and natural resources as well as an individualistic philosophy and political democracy, it seems only to be expected that Britain would be able to push ahead of other nations in industrial and economic development.

In much of Europe, on the other hand, large estates remained important. Governments were absolute monarchies, unlike the limited monarchy of Britain. Excesses of the French Revolution, as we noted, gave new strength to a more conservative outlook. It is thus not surprising that philosophical, political, and economic thought differed markedly from the individualistic philosophy upon which British classical economics was based. To Adam Smith *The Wealth of Nations* was the sum of individual wealth and the nation only an aggregation of individuals. Government functions were to be limited to providing primarily defense and justice.

The European continental school views these issues very differently. Strongly influenced by the so-called Romantic movement, which can be described as a revolt against the material and logical and in favor of the search for the inner spirit and truth of nature and man. German nationalism was one of the "truths" that found its expression in the writings of such Romanticists as Fichte, Hegel, Müller, and List. Acceptance of the ideas encompassed in the Romantic movement led A. H. Müller (1779-1829) and Friedrich List (1789-1846) to criticize the position of Adam Smith and the classical school.

What was the role of the individual in society as viewed by the Romanticists? It differed sharply from that of John Locke, Adam Smith, and their followers. Jean Jacques Rousseau (1712-78) considered the general will or objective of society to be distinct from that of the individual. Montesquieu, in his search for a theory of law, found it in the spirit of the society to which the law applied. Government cannot rule arbitrarily according to Montesquieu. It must rule in the spirit of the society and only as this changed could laws be changed accordingly. To Immanuel Kant (1724-1804) in Germany the concept of duty was important. Men can be free but being free they have a duty to other men. Other Germans such as Johann G. Fichte (1762-1814) and Georg Wilhelm Friedrich Hegel (1770-1831) went further than Kant. Fichte envisioned a moral will behind the individual will—a purpose of the universe, or God, whose will projected itself into individual wills. Hegel in turn developed this concept into a comprehensive view of history, society, and philosophy.

Consider briefly Hegel's philosophy. To Hegel the entire universe was a manifestation of God or the absolute. Its primary purpose was revealed in the human mind. History was the unfolding of this purpose in the external phenomena over time. Human social organizations and their changes were reflected in the evolving ideas in the minds of men through which they sought the will of God. Advancement was attained through a series of struggles between ideas seeking the final truth. This is the familiar Hegelian thesis or theory clashing with its antithesis or objection and emerging finally as a synthesis or solution. Through this struggle man and his institutions are seen as becoming more perfect and more consistent with the ideal.

According to the Hegelian view, man's nature was not to be found in Locke's explanation. Man's purpose was not a bundle of wants whose satisfaction he sought. His purpose was to be achieved through the harmonious development of all his faculties, not only for himself but for society as a whole. True freedom was expressed in association with others in society, including the state itself. A person who had achieved this freedom would express social wants. In effect, his wants were for the things that were for the social good as well. A concept of freedom that involved conflict between individual freedom and society was simply a manifestation of social and ethical immaturity.

To reach the Hegelian ideal an individual must find his place in society and his will or purpose must become the social purpose or social will. To Hegel, existing institutions were to be accepted and used since the true good was achievable within their framework. Hegel's writings are all the more important since they spanned a good part of the revolutionary upheaval and reaction in Europe.

On this score it is also important to note that Marx's social philosophy was also Hegelian in that he accepted Hegel's concept of the wholeness of society as well as his belief that human evolution is to be interpreted as progress toward a goal or ideal. Marx, however, also rejected in an important sense Hegelian philosophy. Unlike Hegel, who underscored the evolution of ideas and perceived the outward phenomena of society as reflecting the progress of ideas, Marx emphasized the outward. According to Marx the course of development of human ideas and social organization was influenced by external and particularly economic factors.

The continental views on property and money are particularly instructive. Rousseau's opposition to property rights as they existed in France are well known. He considered the system in France of his time as an outrage against the rights of man. He too, like Locke, based his property rights theory on the idea of natural rights. Unlike Locke, who used natural rights to justify property rights, Rousseau used natural rights doctrine to condemn the practice of property rights.

This is not to deny Hegel's later view that property rights are integral elements in individual and social development. Rousseau simply underscored the point that in the France of his time many men were excluded from participating in the exercise of property rights. Many were also excluded in Hegel's Germany when he wrote. The reason for their difference evidently was that Hegel unlike Rousseau chose to ignore the reality of the situation.

To Kant property rights were subject to government consent, since individual property rights affected others in society. The government represented these others and thus these rights were within its proper domain. Nevertheless, individual property rights were to be defended on the principle that justice was achieved through inequality of property. They represented rewards to the individual for his contribution to society.

Fichte's and Smith's views on government underscored the differences between the classical and continental schools of thought. In his *Inquiry into the Nature and Causes of Wealth* (Cannon edition, Modern Library p. 657) Smith wrote in 1776 that there were three agenda of government:

1. ... the duty of protecting the society from the violence and invasion of other independent societies ...
2. ... the duty of protecting, as far as possible, every member of the society from the injustice or oppression of every other member of it ...
3. ... the duty of erecting and maintaining certain public works and certain institutions, which it can never for the interest of any individual, or small number of individuals, erect and maintain, because the project could never repay the expense to any individual or small number of individuals, though it may frequently do much more than repay it to a great society.

It is the third item in Smith's statement that could be and indeed is interpreted as a call for a large amount of activity by government. After all there are many projects without prospects of profit to individuals, with social benefits in excess of their social costs. This could amount to a considerable size in the "output mix" for a nation-state —far larger undoubtedly than what Adam Smith had in mind in the third item on his agenda.

Fichte, on the other hand, viewed government as a body with members or organs. It was more than an assembly of individuals as viewed by Smith and Locke. Government was a composite whole in much the same fashion as a human body is composed of its constituent elements. Thus it is that the state cannot be viewed, according to Fichte, as a simple assemblage of individuals any more than could the human body be considered as a collection of cells. In effect, Fichte's "output mix" for a nation-state was more comprehensive and encompassing than that of Smith.

On property rights Fichte argued that an individual possessed such property rights as are useful for the necessities of the state. In effect, the individual must agree to use the property suitably and usefully for the necessities of the state. If he purchased farm lands, for instance, he had to cultivate these lands. Property rights also extended to professions, provided the individual supplied work of sufficient quantity and quality. Thus the links between property rights and social duties were clearly established.

These links between property rights and social duties extend back into the medieval ages and the European guilds and forward into their modern counterparts in Fascist Italy and Nazi Germany. In less extreme form they also exist in the contemporary system of professional organizations throughout the world. There is also a modern counterpart in various manpower planning schemes within central planning organizations in Fichte's argument that it was the responsiblity of the government or its designated bodies to ascertain the manpower requirements of the various branches of the economy. These views are in marked contrast to the individualistic rights as argued by Locke and Smith.

Indeed Hegel's view of property underscored the fact that like other rights, property rights were subject to the sovereignty of the state. It was more than individual possession according to Hegel. It was an expression of personality. In its possession a person became rational. Since the expression of personality through property was beneficial, the state protected it. Moreover, Hegel argued in favor of inequality of property because among persons variously endowed, inequality must occur and equality would be wrong. Justice demands merely, according to Hegel, that every person should have property, not that every man's property should be equal.

Fichte's view on money again contrasted with that of Adam Smith, David Ricardo, and others of the classical school. Money was something more than a means to facilitate exchange. It represented, according to Fichte, a state recognition of its indebtedness to private cash balance holders. Unlike Ricardo, for instance, Fichte did not believe that the state could overissue money. He did not view a general rise in prices as having distributional effects. Many of Fichte's views were incorporated later by Georg Fredrich Knapp (1842-1926) into his *State Theory of Money* (Staatliche Theorie des Geldes). This view on money was also supported by Friedrich von Gentz (1764-1832) and Adam Heinrich Müller (1779-1829).

Though sympathetic to some of Smith's views, Müller did not agree with Smith's materialism. He was much more favorably disposed to the views of Hegel and Fichte on the state and society as constituting a whole. The individual was a part of society in which regard for others was a critical element. Indeed, like Hegel and Fichte, Müller appeared to glorify the political nation-state. It does appear that Hegel, Fichte, and particularly Müller were the ideological forebearers of German National Socialism.

For his part Gentz also appeared to defend feudalism still prevalent in many German states at the beginning of the nineteenth century. Feudalism did not recognize complete property ownership but only rights and associated duties. Thus it fit well into the ideological concept of an organic society. To Müller personal goods were of the same gender. They involved rights and duties to others. The individual thus was not completely his own person since he also had duties to others. Production was important because the supply of goods and services were increased as a result. Müller, however, did more. He included as factors of production the nation's entire spectrum of ideas and cultural capital.

In essence, Gentz, Müller, and others in the continental European school supported the Fichte-Hegel view of society in much the same fashion as Adam Smith produced the economic counterpart of the philosophical individualism of John Locke. There are other important differences between the classical and continental schools. Consider the issue of economic nationalism and protectionism.

Friedrich List (1789-1846) was certainly among the more important contributors to the discussion of economic nationalism and protectionism. His study, *The National System of Political Economy, International Trade, Trade Policy and the German Customs Union* (Das national System der politischen Oekonomie, der International Handel, die Handels Politik und der Deutsche Zollverein) (1841), argued that the economics of Smith and his followers totally ignored the nation-state and its requirements. According to List, societies passed through several historical stages. There was, first, the barbarian or primitive stage. This was followed by the second or pastoral stage. In the third stage a society became self-sufficient in agriculture. The fourth included agriculture as well as manufacturers for local consumption. The fifth state included agriculture as well as manufacturers for world trade.

According to List the full-trade policies advocated by Smith and the classical school were suitable only for countries in the fifth stage.

In List's time such an arrangement was suitable only to Great Britain but not for Germany or the United States. Both countries needed to expand their manufactures in order to reach the stage of development that Great Britain had already achieved. The problem not addressed by Smith and his followers was the policy or policies that each nation must pursue to make progress in their various stages of development. In a completely unified world body of nations, List argued, economic interdependence and specialization could be defended. In reality, however, the possibilities of war and/or interruption of trade among nations was ever present. Moreover, any nation with only agriculture as its industry was depriving itself of the full productivity and output of all its resources.

The policies recommended by List to achieve and develop manufactures in such countries as Germany called for protective import tariffs to be imposed gradually and with care on desired industries so as not to be disruptive to the economy. These duties were to be lowered as the industry in question achieved the necessary maturity to compete. The policies were to be appropriately synchronized to the stage of a country's development.

List's influence on the U.S. protectionist movement is well known; he spent considerable time in the United States. In particular, Henry Carey followed List, calling for a diversified U.S. industry capable of giving employment to all of its diversified resources. His justification, among others, included differences in transportation costs for the development of domestic industry.

Other influential members of the U.S. protectionist movement, among others, included Daniel Raymond (1786-1849), and Alexander Hamilton (1757-1804), best known for his influence in the publication of the *Report on the Subject of Manufactures* in 1791. Among other recommendations the *Report* called for the establishment of a fund that would serve to encourage manufacturing in the United States. The criteria for establishing such manufacturing included the local availability of raw materials as well as demand for the industry's products. Development of manufacutring over agriculture was preferable since manufacturing gave greater scope for the development of labor skills as well as reducing dependence on foreign sources of supply.

List, Hamilton, and other protectionists argued for a more diversified and self-sufficient nation-state, which they felt their policies would bring about. The extensive specialization advocated by Smith and his followers would, according to the protectionists, set the nation-state on a course of economic instability. Specialization, moreover, was risky in terms of a country's national defense. Dependence on foreign sources of supply, which could be cut off, was thus to be discouraged.

The economics of the classical school did not have an enthusiastic following on the Continent. The Europeans and even some Americans tended to prefer the protectionist policies advocated by such writers on political economy as List. Others incorporated what they considered the relevant features of the classical school of economics into a broader study of an integrated and evolving society. The philosophical background for this evolutionary view of economics was provided by Hegel. This was the so-called German historical school of economics, which prevailed on the Continent between 1843 and 1883. Dominant figures in this school included Wilhelm Friedrich Roscher (1817-94), Bruno Hildebrand (1812-78), Karl Gustav Adolph Knies (1821-98), Gustav von Schmoller(1838-1917), and Karl Bücher(1847-1930).

According to the German historical school, economic organization and theory must be related to the environment. On this view classical economics is not of universal application, it is limited to the society in which it emerged. An economics of general application must incorporate a study of the history of various societies and human society as a whole, and such a study must be inductive. Princples are to be found by examining data concerning the environment to which they could be considered to apply. These studies are to be undertaken by economists together with historians and statisticians. Ironically, Adam Smith's *Wealth of Nations* is surely consistent with the objectives and desires of the German historical school, while the works of Ricardo and Nassau Senior (1790-1864) are not.

In particular, those of the historical school disagree with the view of the classical school that enlightened self-interest is the primary economic motive. They argue that human motives are much more complex, so that reasoning based on self-interest is not of general application.

It is from romanticism and Germany that the historical school drawing on Hegelian idealism and the traditionalist reaction to the scientific views of the Enlightenment seeks to trace the slow and inevitable development of human society and institutions from the record of the past. History is looked upon not as a record of the effects of the interplay of complex forces but itself as a force that produced things in accordance with a preordained plan and for the realization of a hidden purpose.

Since the historical school relies for explanation upon a chronological survey of successive facts, it abandons experimental science, in the sense of verifiable cause and effect in its analysis of social institutions. To understand the present and to know how it came about it is only necessary, according to its followers, to know what preceded it in time. The importance of historical development is indeed important in expanding the range of observed phenomena. It is equally, if indeed not more, important, however, to understand the present in its own terms. The historical school simply claims too much. Under the circumstances such enthusiasm is understandable. It did widen the horizon of human intellect by providing critical methods for determining what the past had been. Nevertheless, social paleontology can never take the place of an analysis of contemporary forces and events. History is not a cause but a phenomenon itself to be explained.

NOTES

1. In the mountain of literature on the evolution of ideas, see, for example, Ellis T. Powell, *The Evolution of the Money Market, 1385-1915* (London: Frank Cass, 1966); Warren J. Samuels, "Adam Smith and the Economy As a System of Power," *Review of Social Economy*, October 1973, pp. 123-37; L. Rogin, *The Meaning and Validity of Economic Theory* (New York: Harper & Row, 1958); J. J. Spengler and W. R. Allen, *Essays in Economic Thought* (Chicago: Rand McNally, 1960); George Stigler, *Production and Distribution Theories* (New York: Macmillan, 1941); J. Dorfman, *The Economic Mind in American Civilization*, Vol. 3 (New York: Viking Press, 1949); E. K. Hunt, *History of Economic Thought: A Critical Perspective* (Belmont, Calif.: Wadsworth, 1979); Carl Menger, *Problems of Economics and Sociology* (Urbana: University of Illinois Press, 1963); J. A. Schumpeter, *History of Economic Analysis* (New York: Oxford University Press, 1954); Ludwig von Mises, *The Anti-Capitalistic Mentality* (New York: D. Van Nostrand, 1956); E. J. Hamilton, A. Rees, and H. G. Johnson, eds., *Landmarks in Political Economy*, Selection from the *Journal of Political Economy* (Chicago: University of Chicago Press, 1962); Frank H. Knight, *The Ethics of Competition* (New York: Augustus M. Kelley, 1950); Edmund Whittaker, *Schools and Streams of Economic Thought* (Chicago: Rand McNally, 1961); J. Viner, *Studies in the Theory of International Trade* (New York: Harper and Bros., 1937); D. Vickers, *Studies in the Theory of Money* (Philadelphia: Chilton Co., 1959); George Macesich, *The Politics of Monetarism: Its Historical and Institutional Development* (Totowa, N.J.: Rowman and Allanheld, 1984).

5

RESPONSES: THE NEOCLASSICAL SCHOOL, THE WELFARE STATE, AND JOHN MAYNARD KEYNES

THE NEOCLASSICAL SCHOOL

The rise of socialism, the demand for social justice, and Marx's use of such instruments of the dominant ideology as the labor theory of value and the theory of capital accumulation to attack its legitimacy—all prompted a search for a theoretical defense of the existing system. In part, the new defense presented is that of the philosophy of the individual developed and cultivated largely by dominant business and economic interests from the mid-nineteenth century up to and beyond World War II. In effect it is a reinforced version of the laissez-faire argument discussed earlier in this study.

Economists for the most part did not take the extreme position of individualism very seriously. For one thing, Benthamite utilitarianism suggested that government intervention may on occasion be justified by the greatest-good argument. For another, economists concerned themselves with pressing social issues for which the philosophy of extreme individualism provided little insight. This did not mean, however, that economists rejected the individual philosophy. On the contrary, they remained within its general framework.

More important, economists intentionally or otherwise developed a new theoretical apparatus that presumably serves to refute the Marxian critique of capitalism. This is the neoclassical economics developed since 1870. In effect, the foundation of economics is reduced to the desires and wants of the individual, and the whole theoretical explanation of production, distribution, and prices is based on the single assumption of rational individual self-interest. Neoclassical economics is a significant scientific advance, since it reduces to the simple but elegant idea of marginalism a complex set of separate theories of value, distribution, and returns to factors of production. The value of a product or service is not the result of the amount of labor embodied in it, but of the usefulness of the last unit purchased. With marginalism a new approach to economics developed.

Carl Menger (1840-1921), William Stanley Jevons (1835-82), Leon Walras (1837-1910), and Alfred Marshall (1842-1924) shifted the focus of economics from social classes and their economic interests underscored by David Ricardo and Karl Marx to that of the individual. The individual consumer became a centerpiece to the theoretical apparatus of economics, displacing the principle of income distribution envisioned by Ricardo as the mainspring of economic progress and on which Marx based his theory of the breakdown of capitalism. The system of free markets does maximize individual welfare. Since consumers are assumed to maximize their satisfaction and since production responds to consumer wants, it follows that the result will be welfare maximizing. Moreover, marginalism also shows that the costs of production are pushed to the lowest level possible by competition. If allowed to operate without constraints, the entire economy becomes a pleasure-maximizing machine in which the differences between consumer benefits and production costs are increased to the highest level possible. In short, economics is transformed into a service consistent with the individualist social philosophy of Herbert Spencer and William Summer Graham.

The development served also to reinforce, at least in the United States, the legal theories of U.S. Supreme Court Justice Stephen Field (1816-99) and the philosophy of unrestricted individualism in U.S. constitutional law. One result of Field's interpretation was to eliminate much state legislation dealing with economic affairs, including the regulation of hours of work, child labor, and factory conditions. Private property is thus viewed as a natural right that no government can interfere with lightly.

Marx's challenge is also taken up in the application of marginal analysis to income distribution, which demonstrates that all factors of production—labor, land, and capital—earn a wage exactly equal to their contribution to the value of output. Called the theory of marginal productivity and based on the last marginal unit, its conclusion is that workers would be paid a wage equal to the last unit of output they produced. The same idea is applied to profits earned from capital and to rent from land. In effect, to each factor of production the same law applied. No one could exploit anyone else since everyone received what he deserved. The entire product is exhausted and no surplus value exists. Marx's concerns are simply irrelevant.

This happy state of affairs, critics are quick to point out, depends very much on the assumptions of marginal productivity theory. In the first instance, the theory rests on the assumption of perfect competition. Second, all factors of production must be completely substitutable for one another. Third, there must be no change in costs of production per unit of output as the level of production falls or rises. Not all economists are satisfied by such assumptions. Indeed, some economists have never accepted the theory of marginal productivity, which they view as singularly unreal.

It is the issue of periodic booms and depressions which seems to plague the rapidly industrializing countries, that attracted considerable public and government attention. During the first half of the nineteenth century, little concern was shown by most economists, thanks to their acceptance of the general propositions of Say's Law of Markets, according to which there should be no periodic economic breakdowns and the economy should continue to operate at uninterrupted high levels of output and employment. Say's Law states that demand is created by production, and in the aggregate the two can never get out of phase with one another. Economists interested in business cycles typically sought causes outside the framework of production and distribution.

Stanley Jevons (1835-82), for instance, developed a quantitative relationship between sunspots and business fluctuations, arguing that these fluctuations are connected with "periodic variation of weather affecting all parts of the earth, and probably arising from increased waves of heat received from the sun at average intervals of ten years." This serves simply to reinforce Say's Law, since the "cause" is outside the system of production and distribution. Perhaps the best interpretation within Say's Law is provided by the argument that the monetary system generates instability while the basic system of production and distribution is stable. Stabilize the monetary and financial system, and general economic stability is assured.

In 1873 Walter Bagehot, in his by now classic on money and finance, *Lombard Street*, spelled out how in his view it was to be done: Limit the expansion of credit to legitimate needs of business through effective action by the "central bank." This will prevent excessive credit issue from overstimulating the economy and thus developing into a crisis. Once the situation gets out of hand, the "central bank" can probably moderate the crisis but the economy will simply have to weather out the storm.

These theoretical advances served, among other things, to firmly entrench capitalism and defend it from its critics. Marginal utility, marginal productivity, and the monetary theory of business cycles supplemented the basic analysis of classical economics. The free-enterprise economy is pictured as operating to produce what consumers want, thus maximizing welfare, distributing products justly, and normally operating at full utilization of resources. The issue of laissez-faire in neoclassical economics is not a rigidly held doctrine. In fact, the major area of exception is monetary policy, which is "assigned" to the government and its agent, the "central bank." It is their responsibility to preserve economic stability by properly managing the money supply so as to serve the "legitimate needs of business." This is interpreted to mean the needs of production and distribution. The banking school influence here in the form of the "real bills" doctrine is obvious. Even so, such monetary intervention is to be held to a minimum and strictly guided by the free market. In short, "discretionary" monetary policy is to be limited by the requirements of the free market, and within the constraints imposed upon it by the gold standard. As a result, the scope for the exercise of discretionary authority by central banks is very limited indeed.

Arguments raised in support of the mercantile or banking school tradition are based on two principal ideas. One is that the country's bank money will expand only in proportion to the "needs of trade" if banks restrict themselves to discounting only "real bills of exchange." Converse circumstances will prevail when trade declines. The second presumption, closely associated with the first, is that a country's currency will have a desirable elasticity if only commercial banks will maintain a reasonable liquid reserve position and operate competitively. Before 1860 in the United States and elsewhere, the first idea prevailed; that is, the limiting effect of quality on the quantity of loans was stressed. Thereafter, the quest for elasticity and liquidity dominated the banking scene. These two concepts constitute what economists call the "real bills" doctrine.

Although the rationale of the real bills doctrine has been attacked throughout history by economists and others, it has never been completely vanquished. Indeed, the doctrine is firmly lodged in central and commercial banking practices. Supporters of the doctrine argue that it provides an intrinsic, self-regulating limit to the quantity of bank money. It was the chief support for banking reform in the United States before 1913, and the Federal Reserve Board embraced it after 1913. It is to be found in various "qualitative" control measures over bank credit. It also influences the preferences of central banks for interest rates and money market conditions as policy targets over monetary magnitudes. Neoclassical economists also approve other types of government intervention, which serves to facilitate the operation of free competition and free markets. On this score, concern with monopolies and legislation designed to control their practices tend to be supported by most economists. The fact is that neoclassical economics does not adopt "lock, stock, and barrel" simple individualism and laissez-faire, as critics assert; neither does it opt for wholesale intervention. It does accommodate to realistic needs of society. It does have strong ideological implications, since it serves to rebuild the theory of free private enterprise on a new basis, thereby making the refutation of Marx unnecessary. Private property and free private enterprise weathered the Marxist storm more or less intact, thanks to the efforts of neoclassical economists.

PHILOSOPHY OF THE WELFARE STATE

These issues, however, are not settled to the satisfaction of all concerned. As we noted above, with the close of the nineteenth century, concern about the complex nature of man and his society was simply not adequately addressed by (1) those who argued that society was the sum of individual units that were brought into an easy equilibrium by market forces, and (2) those who argued that the social system was divided into antagonistic classes with social conflict as the source of change. There is a third view, which argues that the chief objective of a society is to promote human welfare. It is, in effect, the philosophy of the welfare state. Its exponents include, among others, such diverse entities as Roman popes, Fabian socialists, New Dealers, and Great Society advocates.

Papal economics attempts to come to terms with the social problems bubbling up from the European industrialization and nationalism that brought about a new socioeconomic and political order to the Continent during the last quarter of the nineteenth century. Pope Leo XIII (1810-1903), in a series of encyclicals issued between 1871 and 1901, opts for the middle ground in the feud between labor and capital. The problem, argues Pope Leo, is not economic but moral. The solution must be based in justice animated by charity. Since these are nonmarket phenomena, they cannot be measured in the market-place in terms of profit and loss, wages and costs.

The papal tilt is at first toward capitalism in the condemnation of socialism and in the defense of private property. Subsequently, a com-promise of sorts came about in an indictment of laissez-faire policies (*On Conditions of Labor*), condemnation of socialism, support for private property rights and the natural rights of individuals. The papal appeal, harking back to theories of Thomas Aquinas of the thirteenth century, criticized extreme individualism of the market economy and called for return to human and community values.

Government intervention is justified, according to papal econom-ics, whenever the welfare and preservation of society is threatened. In these matters justice and fairness are to serve as guides. The tradi-tion established by Pope Leo continued to influence later popes, Ro-man Catholic labor movements, and some political parties. The idea that man and community are one and the emphasis that both individ-ual freedoms and individual welfare are to be reconciled in a society that stresses community values and social justice continues its attrac-tion, in theory if not always in practice.

For instance, Pope John Paul II's encyclical, written during the summer of 1981, is intended to be a kind of sequel to the encyclicals of Pope Leo XIII's "Rerun Novarum" in 1891 and Pope Pius XI's "Quadragesimo Anno" in 1931. Both are powerful social documents, and John Paul's new encyclical is a comprehensive statement on social issues that backs labor unions, urges worker participation in manage-ment, and proposes a "just" family wage and subsidies that would free mothers from the necessity of taking jobs. The encyclical condemns both "rigid" capitalism and the "collectivist system" that eliminates all private ownership of the means of production. It suggests a social-ist middle ground as a model for economic development. The central theme in the 99-page, 22,000-word "Laborem Exercens" ("On Human Work") encyclical is opposition to the "dehumanizing excesses" of modern economic systems.

The encyclical, written in Polish, reflects John Paul's vision of "a just society based on an ideal economic system." John Paul strongly endorses the workers' right to organize unions, to participate to some extent in the management of their companies, and to strike, except for political purposes or in essential public services. Radical and ur-gent changes are necessary to rescue farmers from the big landowners and "to restore to agriculture their just value as a basis for a healthy economy." Multinational corporations are engaged in the condemnable practice of fixing high prices for their products while trying to keep down prices for raw materials and semimanufactured goods, widening the gap between the rich and poor nations. "In order to achieve social justice in the various parts of the world, there is a need for ever-new movements of solidarity of the workers and with the workers," according to Pope John Paul. The encyclical is sure to be studied carefully in the Soviet Union, in the pope's native Poland, and in Latin America and other countries where the Roman church is influential.

While the Papacy grappled with the seeming social, economic, and political chaos in Europe brought about by an industrial society in the late nineteenth century, Fabian socialists John A. Hobson and Richard H. Tawney in England pushed forward ideas and programs to deal with similar concerns. Essentially interventionist, the idea cast government's role as one that assists man in developing his talents to the utmost. This is to be done by government working to remove barriers in man's path to the "good life."

A cascade of social legislation descended upon England as a result. Legislation dealing with factory safety became law in 1891 and 1895; limiting working hours for women and children in 1891; slum clearance in 1890; increased powers for labor unions in 1890-1900; workmen's compensation and child welfare in 1906; old-age pensions in 1908; town planning and redevelopment in 1909; sickness and disability insurance in 1911. In effect, a good deal of welfare legislation—serving as mainstays to contemporary economies—were put into place by the turn of the century.

Even though their vision is behind much English social legislation, such generators and spokesmen of unorthodox ideas as John Hobson received little in the way of gratitude from significant numbers of their contemporaries. In fact, Hobson could not find employment in English universities. Fortunately for Hobson, such of his writings as *Work and Wealth Incentives in the New Industrial Order, Physiology of Industry, Evaluation of Modern Capitalism and Imperialism* did much better. Indeed, V. I. Lenin incorporated into communist ideology Hobson's *Imperialism*, which attacked the selfish expansion of European states.

Similar to Hobson's ideas, Fabian socialists envisioned "a reorganization of society in accordance with the highest moral possibilities" through a democratic socialist regime designed to promote "the greatest happiness of the greatest number." A small but influential intellectual group included such members as George Bernard Shaw, Sidney and Beatrice Webb, H. G. Wells, and Annie Besant. Named after the Roman general Fabius Maximus, "the delayer," who fought Hannibal with guerrilla tactics instead of frontal confrontation, the name signifies the society's philosophy and plan of action. Their vehicle, *Fabian Essays*, established in 1889 under the editorial leadership of Shaw, promoted gradual extension of state intervention in economic affairs to improve working conditions, replace monopoly with government ownership, and promote a more egalitarian distribution of income.

Unlike the Marxists, the Fabians did not view the state as an instrument of class warfare that must be destroyed but rather as a means of social control that, once seized, can be used to promote social welfare. They pushed successfully for the formation of a labor party with a socialist platform in 1906. Their tactics, in effect, involved political action within the framework of democratic, parliamentary government. In short, resort to persuasion rather than revolution was a singular Fabian characteristic. That these efforts bore fruit is indicated by the existence of the British Labour Party and much of contemporary social and welfare legislation in Great Britain.

The economic historian Richard H. Tawney (1880-1963), drawing on past and present world experience, argued for a society reformed along the functional lines of a socialist society. Rewards were to be received by those productive members of society who expended work and effort in the tasks society required and not to such unproductive elements as the promoter, speculator, and rentier who collected large sums of unearned income. Property rights, according to Tawney in *The Acquisition Society* (1920), should not be maintained for which no service is performed. In *Religion and the Rise of Capitalism* (1926), he debated the issue raised by Werner Sombart and Max Weber over whether the Protestant Reformation created the intellectual atmosphere that made possible the rise of modern capitalism. He argued that the two were related, but also that modern society and its business activities were completely amoral. In *Equality* (1931), Tawney's theme was that egalitarianism could support and sustain a democratic political framework. In effect, it was through socialism that human values could receive the necessary development.

The American approach to these same problems of industrialism was characteristically pragmatic, lacking much of the socialist philosophy prevailing in Great Britain and Europe. Workable solutions to specific problems were sought within the traditional framework of American society. Much of the necessary work was attributed to a small group of economists investigating such issues as business cycles, labor relations, monopoly, big business, and social welfare. Through their influence on progressive political leaders at the turn of the century and later the New Deal, they promoted the theme that modern industrial society faced serious problems that would not solve themselves. Government intervention is necessary if the destructive forces of the free market are not to have singularly tragic consequences for both society and the individual.

Thorstein Veblen (1857-1929) represented one of the more important economists in terms of his influence on American reform thought. Essentially, his argument was that fundamental forces of change were at work that required adaptations of the social, economic, and political institutions inevitably opposed by the establishment, and represented by wealth and influence the conflict between change and vested interests. His critique of the "pecuniary society" and the "business system" gave both direction and viewpoint to the movement for economic and social reform. Veblen's two books—*The Theory of the Leisure Class* (1899) and *The Theory of Business Enterprise* (1904)—are considered economics classics.

John R. Commons (1862-1945), along with his followers, formulated specific reform measures and legislation adopted first by some states and later incorporated into the New Deal platform of Franklin D. Roosevelt. Such programs and policies as utility regulation, collective bargaining, and mediation to settle disputes between labor and management on a voluntary basis; unemployment insurance and worker's compensation; promotion of economic growth, employment, and stability are cases in point—clearly a remarkable achievement.

The government, according to Commons, must serve as a mediator between conflicting economic interests and between economic forces and the individual. He did not necessarily reject the view of neoclassical economists that harmony emerges out of the equilibrating forces of the market. The market can reconcile some but not all conflicting interests that arise in such an economy, and government intervention was necessary if equitable solutions were to be obtained.

The New Deal philosophy is essence owed much to Veblen, Commons, and their followers. Through government intervention the public was protected from presumably the worst consequences of an industrial market-oriented society. It represented a singular shift from the view of a harmonious self-regulation free enterprise market-oriented economy as advocated by the classical and neoclassical economists.

The New Deal administration intervention into the economy followed along three paths. One focused on the use of the federal budget to promote adequate aggregate spending in the economy and offset shortfalls in the private sector of the economy. It recognized government responsibility for economic stability in the economy. This recognition was embodied in the Employment Act of 1946 and institutionalized in the Council of Economic Advisors to the president. The second dealt with attempts to promote cooperation between business and labor in various industries. The third dealt with government intervention into regional land-use planning based on water resources—for example, the Tennessee Valley Authority.

Moreover, individuals, according the liberal reform philosphy of the New Deal and in contrast to classical and neoliberal views, do not necessarily contribute most to society by pursuing their own interest nor are they necessarily responsible for all of their misfortune. Society, accordingly, must accept responsibility for the welfare of all individuals so as to enable them to function effectively in society. The passage of such welfare measures as unemployment insurance, workmen's compensation, social security, and federal grants-in-aid in health and education was aimed at providing security for the individual.

In addition businesses are to accept social responsibility beyond mere profitmaking. The pre-New Deal situation whereby, presumably, businesses ran roughshod over human and social values is no longer tolerated. In short, business must justify itself by something more than a profit. What that "something" is, however, is not specified. All of this does not serve to endear the reform liberals to the business community.

The liberal reform philosophy of the New Deal extended into President Truman's Fair Deal, and afterward into the short-lived administration of President Kennedy, to be picked up in the Great Society programs of President Johnson, and essentially carried on through the administrations of Presidents Eisenhower, Nixon, Ford, and Carter. There appears to be a resurgence of neoliberalism and neoclassical economics in the form of "supply-side" economics in President Reagan's administration. The fact is that reform liberalism as manifested in the several past U.S. presidential administrations managed to restructure much of the country's economic and social framework without gross violations of individualism, private property rights, and the market-oriented private enterprise economy.

Events took a less satisfactory course in the USSR and in East European countries during and following the two World Wars. War, revolution, and counterrevolution served to wreck what appeared to be promising liberal reforms that began at the turn of the century and continued, albeit in a halting fashion, into World War I.

At the time, Russia was the most backward country in Europe. It had primitive agriculture and industry staffed, for the most part, by an illiterate population. By professing its allegiance to a Marxist ideology, which postulated that socialism would naturally evolve in highly industrialized economies in which the working class comprised the majority of the population, Russia was simply at odds with received socialist doctrine. The country simply did not square with what Karl Marx and his followers had in mind. To complicate matters, the world revolution had failed and the new Soviet state was surrounded by antagonistic capitalist countries who considered it an "illegitimate child of history."

V. I. Lenin (1870-1924) led the Bolshevik Revolution to a successful conclusion. He did so after convincing his followers that Russia could bypass the capitalist industrial era and move directly from an agricultural, semifeudal society into the socialist era. It was Lenin who formulated the basic idea on how to accomplish the goal of a socialist era. In essence, rapid and large-scale industrialization of Russia would serve as a means for building the working-class society in which socialism could flourish. This required an alliance between workers and peasants under a worker's dictatorship, although priority was given to the construction of an urban and industrial society. Lenin died before his strategy was translated into specific programs of action. A debate on goals and means continued in the 1920s and into the 1930s when Stalin ended discussion with the first of the purge trials that were to shake the very foundations of the new Soviet state.

Joseph Stalin (1879-1953) manipulated the great urbanization-industrialization debate to his favor. The moderates, led by the leading Marxist theoretician Nikolai Bukharin, argued for balanced economic development and the postponement of world revolution until the Soviet state was strong enough domestically to support such a revolution successfully. Although urbanization and industrialization were to be encouraged, it was dangerous for the Soviet state to push the peasants too far and to further threaten their loyalty to the regime. In short, a slower development pace tuned to the realistic possibilities of the Soviet state was prudent. Stalin called this approach the *right deviation*.

Opposing the moderates was the so-called left wing of the Communist Party led by Leon Trotsky (1879-1940), who, in fact, was

Lenin's key man during the Bolshevik Revolution. The idea pushed by the left wing called for mobilizing the country's economy to the utmost, squeezing living standards in order to free resources for industrial development, and using the power of the state to extract the maximum surplus from agriculture, which was to be collectivized and mechanized. In effect, the economy was to be deliberately unbalanced so as to force industrialization. As for the international scene, the Soviet state would never be secure in a capitalist world. As a result, it could best protect itself by exporting world revolution principally by demonstrating the superior productivity of socialism through economic growth.

Stalin, at first, took the position of supporting rapid industrialization and forced-draft development advocated by the left wing, but he ruled against collectivization of agriculture so as not to alienate the peasants. As for world revolution, he sided with the moderates and Bukharin, forming an alliance that drove Trotsky into exile. Whereupon Stalin then sided with the left and opted for collectivization of agriculture, a rapid rate for the accumulation of capital beyond anything called for by Trotsky and his faction. It was also enough to gain for Stalin the support necessary to purge Bukharin. In essence, the debate resolved into the establishment of ambitious development goals and a planning apparatus to carry them out, with the Stalin dictatorship the driving force of the system.

This is the Soviet model with more or less appropriate modification imposed in East European countries following World War II. It is also the model and system dropped by Josef Broz Tito (1892-1980) and Yugoslavia following the Tito-Stalin split in 1948. With the departure of Yugoslavia on its own independent road to socialism in its unique model of "worker-self management," a new chapter in socialism began. The world would not be the same again.

JOHN MAYNARD KEYNES

It is with post-World War I Europe and the Bolshevik Revolution as background that a useful insight is had into John Maynard Keynes's (1883-1946) efforts to formulate new policies designed to preserve and revitalize the market economies of Europe. To Keynes, the challenge was clear enough. The Marxist-Leninist socialists had engineered a revolution that not only brushed aside everything before it but transformed a backward, rural economy into an industrial giant. European civilization, already weakened by war, was now threatened with extinction.

Against the apparent socialist success, Britain continued, as it had in the post-Napoleonic years, a deflationary policy designed to achieve international stability at the expense of internal stability. Keynes argued that Britain's return to the gold standard at the British pound's prewar par would diminish British exports and cause domestic wages, prices, employment, and output to fall, as they had a hundred years before in the post-Napoleonic period because of similar policies. Keynes argued for a managed monetary system in place of the classic gold standard. His advice disregarded, Britain returned to the gold standard, only to realize Keynes's prophecy. The subsequent economic stagnation in Britain, already crippled by war and dissolution of its empire, joined the rest of Europe in waiting for a miracle. In Keynes's view Europe could not afford to wait.[1]

This was Keynes's vision. He lacked, however, a theoretical apparatus to provide a convincing case to an audience educated in classical and neoclassical economics. To demonstrate the futility of the British government's deflationary monetary policy, he had to show the inadequacy of the classical theoretical apparatus that rested on the relationship between the gold standard, the domestic level of employment, and Say's Law of Markets. Keynes realized the need to demonstrate convincingly the relationship between the theory of employment and monetary theory. He devoted more than a decade to the task.

The two-volume *Treatise on Money*, published in 1930, was his first effort to unravel the problem. Essentially, Keynes argues the distinction between investment and savings and their different underlying motivations. Unlike Say's Law, which holds that the two must be equal, Keynes argues that this need not be the case. For instance, if savings are greater than investment, general economic activity will decline; conversely, Keynes's policy prescription, which he argued in the various *Essays on Persuasion*, was similar in the *Treatise* that the monetary system be so managed as to assist in maintaining equality between savings and investment and thereby promoting economic stability. In addition, a program of public works should be put in place whenever called for to reduce undesirable effects of economic depression on employment.

The collapse of the world economy and the onset of the Great Depression of the 1930s created a political and economic environment receptive to new ideas along the lines advanced by Keynes and others. In fact such contributions to economics as those made by members of the National Bureau of Research, the University of Stockholm (Swedish School), including such economists as Knut Wicksell, D. H. Robertson, William T. Foster, W. Catchings, and others, paved the way for the acceptance of Keynes's ideas now presented in *General Theory of Employment, Interest, and Money*, published in 1936. The principles essentially were those he put forward in the *Treatise*. The new development that he added in the *General Theory* was the concept of equilibrium at less than full employment. Accordingly, an equilibrium is possible at a depression level, and unless a change takes place in the relevant variables, the economy will stagnate indefinitely. These ideas stood in direct opposition to the classical and neoclassical theories that dominated economic thought and practice for more than a hundred years.

For practical politicians in search of theoretical justifications for deficit financing already under way in many industrial countries, the *General Theory* came at the right time.[2] It provided a theoretical foundation to the commonsense view that large government expenditures financed by borrowing were needed to ease the hardships of the depression on the population. It appeared to recognize the advantages of the self-adjusting market mechanism argued so eloquently by classical and neoclassical economists, although its important assumption that wages and prices are determined external to the system was at odds with received theory. This is important, for it reinforced the theory's basic interventionist position. It called for the government to manage the general level of economic activity in the interests of society in a manner consistent with individual freedom and a stable social order. In effect, Keynesian economics has provided and articulated the theoretical framework for reform-liberal policies pushed in the United States, Great Britain, and elsewhere since the beginning of the twentieth century. Keynes thus managed to give coherence to his vision and to socioeconomic and political changes accelerated by the tragedies of World War I and the collapse of the world economy in the postwar years.

Correct or not, Keynes offered a politically attractive alternative to receiving theories and policies that appeared detached from reality. This does not mean that other explanations are not consistent with the evidence. I have discussed elsewhere these explanations and will again call attention to a number of them in later chapters of this study.[3]

Thus Keynes and particularly his followers underscore the point that modern society can no longer be left to develop and function without guidance. Accordingly, intelligent control of society's forces is fundamental, and such control must be devoted to the welfare of the entire community. To this end men can discover the best kind of life that can be lived with their resources and their compulsions; they must consciously plan, in light of scientific knowledge and practice, how best to bring it nearer to man. In the hope of meeting this inescapable demand, great nations have unified themselves with fanatical faiths, and have entrusted their destinies to self-appointed elites and dictators. This has had profound influence on advanced nations and the emerging nations of the Third World in the post-World War II era.

It is thus to post-World War I Europe, the Great Depression, and to the events that led to the collapse of the international monetary and financial structure that we can profitably turn for much of the rhetoric and many ideas underpinning policies of the contemporary Third World. National self-determination and the breakup of the Austro-Hungarian Empire created new nation-states in Europe. These nations were, for the most part, relatively small, underdeveloped, ethnically heterogenous, and nationalistic. Located principally in the Balkan and Danubian areas, they drew upon German experience in formulating their development programs and tended toward the interventionist and nationalistic ideas of Frederick List and German romanticism. Industrialization rather than agriculture received priority, with protectionism and particularism rather than individualism, free trade, and cosmopolitanism that the classical and indeed neoclassical school underscored. The importance of industrialization was brought home to the agrarian economies of Europe with the collapse of the international economy and depressed prices for agricultural and raw national commodities.

The central concepts developed for the industrialization of the small agricultural nations in the Balkan and Danubian region of Europe were later carried by emigré scholars to Great Britain and the United States, and ultimately into Anglo-Saxon literature on economic development.[4] Transfer of European ideas gave a nationalistic and interventionist twist to the economic thinking about the development of new nations that does not square perfectly with traditional cosmopolitan free trade ideas of English classical and neoclassical economists. The rise of socialism in the 1930s promoted central economic planning and redistribution of income policies. The Keynesian revolution for its part stressed the failure of the economic system that was avoidable by the application of scientific knowledge. These movements reinforced one another. This in turn led to the view that economic backwardness can be traced to the defects in the private enterprise system and not the backwardness of people and their cultures in relation to the requirements of modern industrial society.[5] Accordingly, development was available to any country willing to drop private enterprise, adopt economic planning, accumulate capital, and invest it to industrialize itself and thus cease its dependence on the agrarian economy. All of this was made to appear possible, moreover, with the

> implementation of social, cultural, and egalitarian restrictions on the freedom of competition and practice of widespread intervention in the process and consequences of industrialization. It suggests that one can have one's cake and eat it too—that there exists some mysterious source of untapped economic energy, which, if liberated can provide both for development and for the liberal fulfillment of other social goals.[6]

These are the antecedents of ideas that serve, in part, the Third World in its drive for independence and development. Great revolutions follow uncharted courses and their final destination is unpredictable. The growing pluralism, diversity, and diffusion of power underscores the inability of the United States and the USSR to shape and control events in the Third World and within their own spheres of influence. The remainder of this study will discuss the limits to the policies of economic nationalism as a means for promoting development and stability in the Third World.

NOTES

1. It is useful here to quote Keynes at length, when he wrote, in 1925:

> On the economic side I cannot perceive that Russian Communism has made any contribution to our economic problems of intellectual interest or scientific value. I do not think that it contains, or is likely to contain, any piece of useful economic technique which we could not apply, if we chose, with equal or greater success in a society which retained all the marks, I will not say of nineteenth century individualistic capitalism, but of British bourgeois ideals. Theoretically at least, I do not believe that there is any economic improvement for which Revolution is a necessary instrument. On the other hand, we have everything to lose by the methods of violent change.
>
> In western industrial conditions the tactics of Red Revolution would throw the whole population into a pit of poverty and death.
>
> But as a religion what are its forces? Perhaps they are considerable. The exaltation of the common man is a dogma which has caught the multitude before now. *Any* religion and the bond which unite co-religionists have power against the egotistic atomism of the irreligious.

The modern capitalism is absolutely irreligious, without internal union, without much public spirit, often, though not always, a mere congeries of possessors and pursuers. Such a system has to be immensely, not merely moderately, successful to survive. In the nineteenth century it was in a certain sense idealistic; at any rate it was a united and self-confident system. It was not only immensely successful, but held out hopes of a continuing crescendo of prospective success. Today it is only moderately successful. If irreligious Capitalism is ultimately to defeat religious Communism, it is not enough that it should be economically more efficient –it must be many times as efficient.

[J. M. Keynes, "A Short View of Russia," *Essays in Persuasion* (New York: Harcourt, Brace and Company, 1932), pp. 306-07].

According to Keynes (ibid., pp. 308-09), the moral issue of the age

is concerned with the love of money with the habitual appeal to the money motive in nine-tenths of the activities of life, with the universal striving after individual economic security as the prime object of endeavor, with the social approbation of money as the measure of constructive success, and with the social appeal to the hoarding instinct as the formation of the necessary provision for the family and for the future. The decaying religions around us, which have less and less interest for most people unless it be as an agreeable form of magical ceremonial or social observance, have lost their moral significance just because—unlike some of their earlier versions—they do not touch in the least degree on these essential matters. A revolution in our ways of thinking and feeling about money may become the growing purpose of contemporary embodiments of the ideal. Perhaps, therefore, Russian Communism does represent the first confused stirrings of a great religion.

2. See also the interesting discussion in W. R. Allen, "Irving Fisher, FDR, and the Great Depression," *History of Political Economy*, Winter 1977, pp. 560-87. Indeed, John Kenneth Galbraith wrote:

By common, if not yet quite universal agreement, the Keynesian revolution was one of the great modern accomplishments in social design. It brought Marxism in the advanced countries to a halt. It led to a level of economic performance that now inspires bittered conservationists to panegyrics of unexampled banality. For a long while, to be known as an active Keynesian was to invite wrath of those who equate social advance with subversion. Those concerned developed a habit of reticence. As a furtive consequence, the history of the revolution is, perhaps, the worst-told story of our era.

[John K. Galbraith, "Came the Revolution" (Review of Keynes's General Theory), *New York Times Book Review*, May 16, 1965.]

Useful on this score are sections of the four essays published by *The Economist* to commemorate the century of J. M. Keynes's birth: Milton Friedman, "A Monetarist Reflects," *The Economist*, June 4, 1983, pp. 17-19; F. A. Hayek, "The Austrian Critique," *The Economist*, June 11, 1983, pp. 39-41; Paul Samuelson, "Sympathy from the Other Cambridge," *The Economist*, June 25, 1983, pp. 19-21; and John Hicks, "A Skeptical Follower," *The Economist*, June 18, 1983, pp. 17-19.

3. See George Macesich, *The International Monetary Economy and The Third World* (New York: Praeger, 1981), especially Chapter 2.

4. See Harry G. Johnson, "The Ideology of Economic Policy in the New States," *Chicago Essays in Economic Development*, edited by D. Wall (Chicago: University of Chicago Press, 1972), pp. 23-40. Johnson cited influential economists in this group, including Mandelbaum, Kaldor, Rosenstein-Rodan, and Balogh. In the case of Balogh, Johnson (p. 30) wrote:

> Balogh's intellectual history and writings are particularly interesting in this respect: a fairly simple conceptual framework, translating into economic language the power politics of the 1930s relationship between Hungary and Germany, is turned successively to the war and post-war relationship and the United Kingdom (and Europe in general) to the United States, then (briefly) to the rivalry between Britain and Germany in post-war Europe, and subsequently to the relationship between the less developed and the advanced countries.

See also Macesich, *The International Monetary Economy*.

5. Johnson, *Chicago Essays*, p. 35.

6. Ibid.

6

THE THIRD WORLD: ECONOMIC AND SOCIOCULTURAL CONSTRAINTS

THE ISSUE

Theoretically it is possible that nationalism can serve to break the crust of tradition and conservatism, thereby accelerate change, and thus promote economic development. In practice, however, the evidence suggests that nationalism does not so much promote development per se as it turns political power into wealth and prestige for the country's elite and bureaucracy at the expense of the rest of the population. The tasks before these countries are truly formidable if nationalism and development are to be judged in Western terms. What many of them lack is virtually everything necessary to a high standard of economic productivity; the injection of nationalism has simply proved for the most part to be both wasteful and disappointing. This chapter discusses important internal economic and sociocultural constraints on economic development and nation-building in the emerging Third World nations.

ECONOMIC CONSTRAINTS

Though growth rates in many of the Third World nations in the 1960s were higher than those in industrial nations, the result was a widening gap between rich and poor on an unprecedented scale. In 1800, at the onset of the Industrial Revolution, the difference in income per capita between rich and poor countries was around 1:2, and countries like India and China were renowned for their riches and wealth. By 1945 the gap had widened to 1:20; by 1965 it was 1:40, and one-sixth of the world's population enjoyed over 70 percent of its real income. By 1975 GNP per capita in the United States was over $6,500, in India it was around $130, and in other countries less than $50. Indeed, no less than 17 countries with a total population of over 200 million still had a GNP per capita of less than $70.

The gross national product in GNP per capita is, of course, a rough indicator of comparative wealth. It does, however, confirm other indexes of development such as literacy, infant mortality, birth rate, and life expectancy. Taken together, these indexes indicate that the international economy between countries operates unevenly. Thus in 1975 more than 60 percent of the world's population—mostly in Africa, Asia, and Latin America—were below the $500 per capita GNP taken as an indicator between absolute poverty and minimal sufficiency.

Perhaps even more important, there is inequality in the annual per capita growth between the developed industrial countries and the Third World. In the period 1950-60, the developed industrial countries grew at an average rate of 2.0 percent a year, whereas the rate for the underdeveloped countries of the Third World was 2.4 percent; in the 1960-70 period, the developed countries of the Third World grew at an average rate of 3.9 percent per year, whereas the rate for the underdeveloped countries was 2.6 percent. In effect, the gap between the developed countries and the underdeveloped Third World is widening.

Indeed, by 1972 the gap between the rich and poor nations was becoming a central issue in international politics. A shift in the balance of power in favor of Third World countries in the United Nations by the late 1960s assured that the issue will remain a focal point in the world. The drift in favor of these nations in the United Nations became clear by the 15th General Assembly (1960-61) when the Afro-Asian countries had a permanent majority. As early as the Bandung Conference in 1955, they had begun to cooperate as a bloc. When the U.N. Conference on Trade and Development (UNCTAD) was established in 1963,[1] these nations transferred their activity to the UN General Assembly.

At the outset UNCTAD's purpose was threefold: increase financial and economic assistance from the rich nations; remove tariff and trade barriers to Third World exports; and establish international commodity agreements to protect the poor countries against fluctuations in commodity prices. The first three UNCTAD meetings—in 1964,

1968, and 1972—were not very fruitful except to vent the dissatisfaction of the Third World with its conditions. After 1972, and especially after October 1973 and OPEC's successful oil price hikes, OPEC's experiment suggested to the Third World a possible model for extracting price increases for its commodity exports from the rich nations. Other raw material cartels such as for copper (CIPEC, 1967), bauxite (IBA, 1974), tin (ITC, 1971 and 1976), rubber (ANRPC, 1970), and iron ore (AIOEC, 1975) operate so as to assist raw material producers in raising prices. Phosphate producers, which include six producers controlling 60 percent of world output, are not organized into a formal cartel, but they did manage to raise prices threefold in 1973 and by a further 50 percent in 1974. On the other hand, mercury producers—headed by Nigeria, Mexico, Canada, and Algeria—formed a cartel in 1974 and raised prices by only one-sixth.

The apparent success of OPEC stimulated the Third World nations to issue a "declaration" for a New International Economic Order (NIEO) at a special session of the United Nations on May 1, 1974. On December 12, 1974, this was supplemented by a "Charter of Economic Rights and Duties" adopted by 120 votes to 6 with 10 abstentions. The stated purpose of NIEO is to assist developing countries, among other things, to secure control over their own resources without interference of the rich countries and of multinational corporations. The United States, among other countries, objected to such an arrangement. Support, however, was obtained from OPEC members at the Algiers Conference, which enabled the Third World nations to maintain a common front at the Seventh Special Session of the United Nations in September 1975. Although very little was achieved, outlines of new and potentially powerful alignments on the international scene were indeed taking shape. The Third World is determined to obtain active, full, and equal participation with the developed industrial countries in the formulation and application of all decisions that concern the international community.[2]

In considering the development gap and especially in appreciating the magnitude of the problem, it is useful to compare and contrast the circumstances in the Third World today with those of the developed countries at the time of their "take off" into sustained economic growth. I have discussed elsewhere the unfortunate coincidence of troubles that brought the collapse of the interwar monetary and financial organizations.[3] Let me turn now to the fortunate coincidence of circumstances that thrust these Western market-oriented countries into sustained economic growth. These fortunate circumstances are by and large economic, political, sociological, and technological.

Consider first the economic circumstances, which can be summarized as capital accumulation, population growth, natural resources, and technological advance. Theories of economic development, in essence, provide us with scenarios about the interrelationships of these factors. They attempt to explain economic growth in terms of some causal factors. They differ from models of growth that take economic growth as given and simply work out the implications of particular kinds of behavior that are postulated but not, typically, explained.

In terms of capital accumulation, net savings and investment in developed countries today averaged 10 to 20 percent of national income during their periods of rapid development. For many Third World countries net savings and investment today is in the range of 5 to 10 percent of national income. Thanks to low levels of national incomes in these countries, there is not enough to provide a critical level of savings and investments necessary to surmount the problem of their economic development.

On the issue of population growth, the developed countries were thrust into development long before they had their population explosion. The Third World countries, on the other hand, have already experienced, indeed are experiencing, population explosions before they are firmly launched into development.

In fact, Simon Kuznets underscores six significant differences between the now-developing countries and developed countries when they began their development:[4] (1) the present level of per capita product in the underdeveloped countries is much lower than it was in the now-developed countries with the possible single exception of Japan; (2) the supply of land per capita is much smaller in the developing countries currently than it was in the present advanced countries when they began their development; (3) agricultural productivity in developing countries today is probably lower than it was in the advanced countries in the past; (4) the inequality in the distribution of income is wider today than in the past, but not in the way that favors accumulation of productive capital; (5) the social and political structure of the low-income countries currently is a much greater barrier than it was in the past; (6) most of the present-day underdeveloped countries are attempting development after a long period of colonial status, whereas many currently developed countries launched development after many years of political independence.[5]

Natural resources and technological advance are other elements with which some Third World countries are in difficulty. Both elements require entrepreneurship if they are to be properly developed and effectively introduced into the economy. Unfortunately, the entrepreneurial spirit appears limited—at least by comparison to the upsurge of enterprise that characterized contemporary developed countries during the eighteenth and nineteenth centuries. Attempts by government to replace private enterprises as innovators and entrepreneurs have not been met with ringing success. The human capital so necessary for the implementation and generation of technological progress and economic development is, simply, in very short supply in the Third World.

Though it may be possible to accelerate technological advance so as to aid development in the Third World, it is not likely that the fortunate coincidence of circumstances that so favored the developed countries of today will be repeated. Populations that grew from levels below optimum in the developed countries and so stimulated development have thus far had a retarding effect on development in the Third World. Technological advance, which is by and large concentrated in the developed countries, is not in tune with the needs and requirements of the Third World.

Political as well as economic factors combined in the eighteenth and nineteenth centuries to assist the contemporary developed countries as I have discussed elsewhere in this study. Consider, for instance, that the significant role that Great Britain played in the nineteenth century in assisting these countries is all too often brushed aside in the Third World's condemnation of imperialism and colonialism. It is useful to compare the policies of the United States and the Soviet Union in the postwar period already discussed with that of Great Britain, particularly after the Napoleonic Wars and the Congress of Vienna in 1815.[6]

In foreign investment it was estimated in the early 1950s that if the United States, for instance, were to lend abroad on a scale equivalent in terms of per capita real income to that of Great Britain during the nineteenth century, it would have had in 1952 $600 billion of foreign investment on which it would have earned $30 billion a year.[7] At the peak of empire in the last third of the nineteenth century, Great Britain invested about 40 percent of its savings abroad. Comparable U.S. capital outflow would be about $30 billion a year as contrasted with an actual net private outflow of some $1 to $3 billion. Prior to World War I, Great Britain obtained about one-tenth of its income from returns on overseas investment. British investment during the pre-World War I period was roughly twice the French and more than twice the German. More than half of British foreign investment was outside the empire, especially in the United States and Latin America.[8]

At the same time, Great Britain actively followed a policy of free trade in contrast to the relatively high tariff policy of the United States. One can argue that Great Britain followed a policy of free trade for reasons of good state policy. It had virtually a monopoly on manufactured products while enjoying nearly a monopsony in the purchase of raw materials and food from abroad. Such a "monopoly-monopsony" position, however, is not enjoyed by the United States—a fact that explains in part the U.S. tariff policy. Great Britain's policy of free trade may have served to accelerate development abroad, whereas U.S. protectionist policy may serve to retard such developments.

Though British private investment abroad was dominant, it was consistent with British government policy. Thus one can argue that the French Revolution provided the British government with an incentive—if indeed not fear—to treat the average British citizen to more consideration than he had received in the past lest he, too, revolt.[9] One way, of course, was to obtain cheap food from abroad. Frontier developments using British capital made cheaper food possible. In effect, assisting economic development abroad was not only good economics but good politics as well.

So, too, with the motivation behind a significant fraction of U.S. government-to-government aid in the immediate postwar period. Various commentators have examined these motivations, ranging from underlying humanitarian impulses of the wealthy U.S. society, on one extreme, and the direct lure of increased export markets on the other. Essentially, however, the consensus places greatest emphasis on the importance of U.S. political and security interests in the Cold War confrontation with the Soviet Union. This is consistent with the concentration of 80 percent of total U.S. aid on countries around the periphery of the Soviet Union and its friends. Moreover, aid programs were (still are?) invariably presented to the U.S. Congress as measures designed to prevent one or another country from falling to Soviet infiltration or takeover. Note is also taken of the fact that the sizes of the aid packages have tended to fluctuate together with the intensity of U.S.-Soviet rivalry. Aid-giving is thus viewed basically as a product of enlightened self-interest.

There is, moreover, the fact stressed by some observers that Great Britain in its dealings abroad did so largely with its own citizens so that physical and political control followed overseas investment.[10] In any case, the other major world powers such as France, Germany, the Netherlands, and Austria-Hungary had an interest in preserving peace and tranquillity in the then developing regions. In contrast, today political control of investment across national frontiers is very difficult to exercise. Competition between the United States and the Soviet Union for friends and influence in the Third World assures something less than tranquillity in the developing countries, even though the stated goal is their growth and stability.

SOCIOCULTURAL CONSTRAINTS

The developing countries of yesteryear, as we have discussed, were much more similar in their sociocultural make-up to those that were developed. They shared attitudes, values, language, and by and large responded to the same incentives as the then developed countries such as Great Britain. Today the situation is very different. The one characteristic they all share is diversity.

The sociocultural environment of a country includes language, religion, values and attitudes, education and technology, and laws, among other important elements. As for culture, it is a durable concept. It is incorporated into the disciplines of anthropology, sociology, political science, history, geography, and economics.[11]

Language

Consider the issue of language and whether a country is homogeneous or heterogeneous linguistically. Though linguistic heterogeneity is not a necessary condition for underdevelopment (witness, for example, developed Switzerland and Belgium), more than 60 of the current developing countries do not share a common language.[12] The fact is that multiplicity of languages in a country tends to hinder economic integration and market size, thereby reducing the division of labor and the possibilities for economies of scale. This also may result in fragmentation of political life and perhaps lead to internal instability. Indeed, scholars have often commented on the fragile nature of heterogeneous societies, particularly when such societies are placed under pressures of rapid development.[13]

India, for instance, is an example of linguistic heterogeneity and its associated problems.[14] No less than 15 major languages are listed along with several hundred other languages of varying degress of importance. Fortunately, many of these language groups are concentrated in compact regions and organized into constituent states of a federation.

Obviously aware of the difficulties presented by linguistic plurality, many developing countries have opted for the promotion of a uniformity strategy by using a single official language for administration, usually inherited from the colonial power. This option, too, has problems, since the former colonial powers typically promoted uniformity by using their own language as the official language.

Indeed, the newer states in Africa and Asia are confronted with the practical issue of what to do about the foreign official language inherited from the colonial power. On the one hand, there are strong reasons against maintaining the colonial language. One issue is that language is a symbol of national identity and independence. Another issue is that the colonial language is often associated with antidemocratic elements of the past. More important is the view that the colonial language may hinder communication between authorities and the rest of the population and so create a barrier for carrying out various development programs. Another is that education is best carried out in the mother tongue. Finally, a foreign language may also be a barrier to development of a nation's cultural life. Still other reasons could be added for discouraging continuation of the foreign colonial language.

Nonetheless, there are also powerful reasons for maintaining the colonial language. One, of course, is simple inertia, because the language has typically been around for a good many years, especially with the elite, the bureaucracy, higher education, and other important elements in the life of a nation. There is, in addition, the practical issue of finding a suitable substitute language, since choosing one of perhaps several tongues in a country presents other problems. Moreover, the former colonial language is typically a modern language capable of meeting the requirements of modern commerce, industry, technology, and education in general, thereby providing the country with access to the sinews of development.

The pressure of events usually forces the developing countries to opt for one of the world's major languages, typically English. There are, however, strong counterpressures in the form of cultural independence and national identity. The resolution of these problems is not easy—certainly not for a fledgling nation in the first euphoria of independence.

The adoption of English, if not as the country's primary language certainly as its second language, has much to recommend to a nation aspiring to participate in the world economy. It is not only a legacy of the British Empire but also from U.S. economic, technological, and military power, especially in the post-World War II era. Indeed, more people in Europe speak English as a second language than any other language, including French.[15]

As a matter of fact, the important role of English in the service of the Third World was provided at the Bandung Conference in 1955, where it was the official language. Indeed, the Soviet Union and China, among others, beam their broadcasts to the Third World in English. English, then, is an important factor in aiding development in the Third World, just as it had been for more than a hundred years in the British dominions and the United States.

Religion

The importance of religion in the cultural environment and indeed as a determinant in many of the external manifestations of culture should not be minimized. Much behavior can in one way or another stem from the religion of the country's culture, for example, role of women, educational systems, social relations, and political organization. The Judeo-Christian tradition and ideas contained in the Reformation and the Calvinist and Puritan ethic were shared by the developing Western countries of 200 years ago. Today the situation is very different.

Consider the effects that five of the major religions—Animism, Hinduism, Buddhism, Islam, and Christianity—have on economic behavior and the economy of the Third World. A quick survey will suggest that in terms of per capita income the world's Protestant nations have the highest, followed by the Catholic countries. The Muslim nations are in the next category, with the Buddhist and Hindu countries in the bottom group.[16] The animistic or nonliterate religious societies (largely in Africa) are more mixed in that literate religions such as Christianity or Islam coexist.

The role of religion in economic development has been treated by many scholars so that there is little point in reporting their results except to emphasize that religion is important even in so-called sectarian societies. It affects a society's values, attitudes, achievements, and motivation in general. Its divisive nature is also only too visible in countries torn apart through religious heterogeneity such as in

Northern Ireland between Protestants and Roman Catholics and in the Indian subcontinent between Muslims and Hindus. No continent is spared the tragedy of religious clashes—witness Muslim pressures on Christians in Africa and the Arab and Jewish tragedy in the Near East.

Animism

Let us then examine briefly the five major religions noted above insofar as they impinge on economic development. Consider, first, Animism, thought by many to be mankind's oldest religion. It is variously described (for example, "primitive religion" or "nonliterate religion") as the view of nature as animated by indwelling spirits. This appears to have preceded the view of religion as controlled by external deities or, in effect, Animism precedes Deism.[17] More than 30 developing countries in the Third World can cite Animism as a major religious factor. Most of these countries are located in Africa, south of the Sahara. Five are in Latin America, where they are mixed with Roman Catholicism. The only Asian country listed is Laos, where Buddhism is dominant.

The important point is that animistic societies tend to be strongly conservative and tradition oriented. As a result new products and techniques are not easily adopted. Efforts to introduce new methods into agriculture, for instance, will quite likely meet strong resistance. Moreover, the belief in "magic" in these societies limits the appeal of science and indeed the scientific method requiring a vast and expensive reeducation program if development is to take place with modern techniques. It should be no surprise that these societies are also the least developed in the Third World.

Hinduism

Hinduism is difficult to describe as a religion, and it is often called "a way of life." As a result it is even more difficult to change since one is not confronted with a religious dogma but instead with a way of life developed over a period of more than 4,000 years on the Indian subcontinent.[18] To understand India one must attempt to understand Hinduism, since more than 80 percent of the total population of over 500 million are Hindus.

Although the practice of Hinduism varies widely from class to class and from region to region, several issues do stand out. For instance, unlike Christianity and Islam, Hinduism is not a creedal religion. This means that practices tend to be important. Intuition, experience, and inward realization are more important than intellect, dogma, and outer experience in Hinduism. Its strength and durability is the ability to assimilate and adapt to become "all things to all men."

The impact of Hinduism on the economy cannot be very positive. For instance, the caste system, which was originally a color bar, is tied up with labor mobility between occupations. But the caste and subcaste system is more than simply occupation or indeed social class as these terms are normally understood. The differentiation is much stronger. Perhaps a better descriptive word is "species." Legislation such as in the Indian Constitution outlawing discrimination based on caste does not always change social behavior, whose roots are deep in its history.

The extended family or "Baradari" is a source of stability and strength in Indian society. Many enterprises, for instance, are family endeavors and are based on family relationships rather than on modern Western organizational concepts. Nepotism in India has a positive value. Consumption, too, is a joint-family issue, unlike the Western single-family or household unit.[19] It would be inaccurate, however, to argue that modernization under Hinduism is impossible. Witness, for example, India's two centuries of progress and development—to be sure under British influence.

Progress, nevertheless, has resulted in creating a Hindu elite capable of sustaining such progress. D. K. Rangnekar aptly summarized the Indian problem in the following:

> The Young Indian must come round to a rational and objective view of material advancement. He must be able and willing to tear himself away from family ties; flout customs and traditions; put economic welfare before cow worship; think in terms of farm and factory output rather than in terms of gold and silver ornaments; spend on tools and training rather than on temples and ceremonials; work with the low caste rather than starve with the high caste; think of the future rather than of the past; concentrate on material gains rather than dwell on Kismet (destiny). These are extremely difficult changes to envisage in the Hindu social structure and ideas. But they seem unavoidable.[20]

Buddhism

In contrast to the complexities of Hinduism, Buddhism is relatively simple and straightforward in teaching and practice. This does not mean that diversity does not exist in Buddhism, for it most certainly does as in all major religions. Two divisions of Buddhism (Theravada Buddhists in South and East Asia and Mahayana Buddhists in North Asia) number about 200 million people. As with Hinduism, so too with Buddhism it is more than a religion in the Western sense. It is a life-style, an all-encompassing element of spiritual, cultural, and political identity. Buddhism emphasizes wantlessness and contemplation rather than consumption and work.[21] Though it may not be world-denying, it is questionable how world-affirming Buddhism is in terms of economic development. For instance, the Buddhist countries of Southeast Asia are among the least developed members of the Third World.

In the Northern Asian countries of China, Japan, Korea, Mongolia, Tibet, and Nepal, where Mahayana Buddhism exists, it does so alongside Taoism and Confucianism in China and Shintoism in Japan. As a result, Buddhism is diluted and modified and its impact on the economies of these countries is difficult to ascertain.

Islam

No single event in world history druing the millennium between the fall of Rome and the European voyages of discovery was more significant than the rise of Islam. Thanks to OPEC and oil, Islam is again a force to be reckoned with and so has drawn particular world attention. It is the religion of more than 500 million people, the majority living in the Third World and primarily in Asia, the Middle East, and Africa. In Europe and other regions it is a minority religion. Conquest and the force of arms account for its spread, though Islam's proffered absence of racial discrimination very likely had appeal, especially in India, where most of the converts were of lower caste. Brotherhood and equality as preached by Islam proved attractive in other places as well.

Strong as Islam's appeal is in the Third World countries, it, too, is more than a religion; it is also legislation that organizes all human relationships. The *Sharia* or law of Islam includes every detail of human life—not only the state organizations, but also personal and social relations and actions. Unlike other countries, Muslim nations are established as religious states wherein each citizen accepts full responsibility for the performance of his religious duties and observance of the *Sharia*. No distinction in Muslim countries exists between the secular and religious. Indeed, the Muslim name for citizen is *mukallaf*, which means one who accepts responsibility for carrying out duties laid out by the *Sharia*.

No formal clergy exists in Islam, only scholars who are experts in the sacred book of Koran and Traditions (Hadith) that have grown up alongside it. These influential scholars, or *ulama* (or *ulema*) as they are called, play a very important role as both teachers and preachers. One result of such influence is that *ulamas* may serve to provide or discourage change and so encourage or retard economic development.

The foundations of Islam rest on five pillars:

1. The Profession of Faith: "There is no God but Allah, and Mohammed is His prophet."
2. Prayer: Practiced five times a day, according to a set ritual.
3. Fasting: Done during daylight hours in the month of Ramadan.
4. Almsgiving: One traditionally donates a portion of one's income.
5. The hajj: A pilgrimage to Mecca is made once during one's lifetime.

To judge from available evidence, Muslim countries tend to be in the lower end of economic development. Those with oil resources, of course, are experiencing a significant period of growth in GNP as well as general revival. Other indicators of development, however, tend to confirm the general backwardness of these countries. For instance, the literacy rate is significantly below 50 percent; so, too, is newspaper circulation. Population density is low and so is the productivity of agriculture. The general picture, in effect, is one of general rural backwardness with a high percentage of the population engaged in primitive agriculture. This is sad commentary indeed for the fact is that from the ninth to the fourteenth centuries Muslim teachers and researchers kept alive and extended the range of Greek science and strengthened the bases of modern science.

Insallah, or "God willing," is the orthodox belief that everything, good or evil, proceeds directly from the divine will, being irrevocably recorded on the Preserved Tablet. This sort of fatalism, along with the pervasive impact of Islam, is considered by many observers as the major cause for the lack of economic progress in Muslim countries. For instance, *Insallah* conflicts with the idea of insurance, which can be viewed as working against Allah's will. As a result, world banks may find themselves financing uninsured projects, including inventories. So, too, is the prohibition against charging interest for loans, though this is typically circumvented by charging commission instead. However, if a bank must go to court to collect, it may well be faced with a Muslim court decision awarding only the loan principal.

Islamic countries, in essence, are at a crossroads today. They must choose whether to deny the essentials of Islam and opt for a secular state or to go through the difficult struggle of trying to produce an Islamic order or an Islamic state. The struggle is reminiscent of the conflicts between the Medieval Roman Church and the emerging European nation-states as we discussed. Indeed, Islam is 600 years younger than Christianity. These choices will not be made easier by a leadership split among professional politicians, who are essentially secular, Westernized, and non-Islamic and who simply jump on the Islamic bandwagon to achieve political goals.

The *ulama* constitute the second group who are for all practical purposes professional men of religion. They are conservative traditionalists, who have nonetheless committed themselves to the preservation of Islam so that it is, in fact, a living tradition. They are to be found in the political, cultural, and educational life of all Muslim countries. Moreover, they are organized and their efforts are productive: for instance, such organizations as the Nahdatuh ulema in Indonesia; in Pakistan the Jamaat i Ulema i Islam and the Jamaat i Ulema i Pakistan; in Cairo the sheiks of Al Azlar; in Morocco the Rahitat Ulema al Maghreb; finally the entire body of sheiks in countries such as Saudi Arabia, which claim to be Islamic states.

Another group, though presumably Westernized, are really not Westernizers so much as they are modernizers. They claim to be Islamic believers but reject the more fundamentalist interpretation. They appear to be the most serious and most important factor in the upsurge of Islam in the post-World War II period. They have taken upon themselves to rethink Islam in modern terms. Such groups as the Moslem Brotherhood in Egypt, the Party for the Liberation of Islam in Jordan, the Jamaat i Islami of Pakistan, the Masjumi Party in Indonesia, the Istiqlal Party in Morocco, the Iran Liberation Movement of Iran, as well as the Mujahidin Al Khalk in Iran; some would also include Colonel Qaddafi of Libya.

These people and organizations vary widely in their approach and objectives. Some want an Islamic society within an Islamic state based on the Koran and the Sunnah; others want an Islamic society within an Islamic order, derived from the Koran and the Sunnah; some accept violence and others do not. The element that seems to unite all these elements is the desire to make Islam relevant to the contemporary world.

Education, however, is the most critical element in any successful Islamic thrust into the post-World War II world. It is also the issue on which the former colonial powers regarding their Muslim subjects appear to have agreed—namely to give their colonial subjects as little as possible and if at all the wrong kind. The introduction of wholly Westernized and wholly European education systems buttressed by European languages was aimed at providing a minimal colonial administration. The minorities were largely ignored so that those aspiring such education went abroad. They returned as aliens in their own societies.

The most significant change in these societies in the postwar period is that their educational systems at all levels have once again reinstituted in the curricula the teaching of Islam. It is this Islaminization of the young coupled with the shedding of colonial authority that has again brought Islam into confrontation with the rest of the world.

Indeed, confrontation between Islam and the rest of the world has been an on-again, off-again issue for almost 1,500 years. We need but recall the Crusades of the eleventh and twelfth centuries; the Moors in Spain; the fall of the Serbian Empire at the Battles of Marica in 1371 and Kossovo in 1389, which opened Europe to Ottoman incursions; the fall of Constantinople in 1453 to the Muslims, which marked the end of the Byzantine Empire; the establishment by Charles V in 1521 of a Military Frontier running through current-day Yugoslavia and lasting until 1871 as a defense and containment of Islam; the Ottoman Empire, which included a significant portion of Europe and whose rise encouraged the great European voyages of exploration in search of alternative trade routes to the East in much the same way as today's search for alternative sources of energy; the Balkan Wars of the nineteenth and early twentieth centuries as well as World War I owe their genesis in some part to Islamic incursions into Europe; the Greek and Turkish conflicts; the Russian experience with Islam over the centuries also colors today's response to its resurgence in the Islamic countries of Asia, the Middle East, and Africa.

The Third World movement since World War II is in good measure propelled by Islam located in the Afro-Asian countries. In fact, without its Afro-Asian contingent and especially its oil-rich OPEC members, the Nonaligned Movement as a group of nations would have a difficult time remaining together as the Economic Group of 77. Without the Group of 77 the North-South dialogue and demands for a New International Economic Order would very likely fall on deaf ears.

The Soviet Union, for its part, may have more than 40 million Muslims in Soviet Central Asia and the Caucasus. Though skepticism exists, Soviet incursions into Afghanistan may be explained by a desire to put down the chaos and the spread of Islamic fundamentalism and disintegration in terms of geopolitical and strategic requirements of a historic buffer region. In effect, the spread of volatile, chaotic, unpredictable Islamic anticommunism across Iran, Pakistan, and

Afghanistan could very well open up the whole region and thrust the United States and even Chinese power to the frontiers of the Soviet Union. At the same time, a Soviet thrust south would place it astride the region, eliminating security dangers and achieving a time-honored desire of commanding a position in the Indian Ocean and the oil-producing area of the Persian Gulf.

Though the Muslim population's challenge to the Kremlin may not be serious thus far, one can speculate about the future, especially in view of Soviet efforts to involve Muslims more actively in decision-making. An educated Muslim elite together with pressure from a high Soviet Muslim birthrate, which if it continues will make Muslims about one-quarter of the Soviet population by the end of the century, spells a very potent force indeed—all the more so if coupled with Islamic nationalism. How to counter Islamic nationalism in the Soviet Union may be one of the most serious problems confronting Kremlin leadership to date.

Yugoslavia seems to have done much better in arranging for its Muslim population of 3 million—the result of the high tide of Islamic expansion into Europe. The fact that Yugoslavia has done so places it in good standing in the leadership of the Third World. There are about 1.7 million Bosnian Muslims in Yugoslavia with the majority living in the republic of Bosnia-Herzegovina. They are descended from Slavs who embraced Islam after the Turkish conquest of Bosnia in 1463. Another 1.3 million are non-Slav Muslims. In 1968 Muslims were given full nationality status, on a par with the Serbs, Croats, Macedonians, Slovenes, and Yugoslavia's other nationalities. Many mosques have been built in Bosnia-Herzegovina, partly financed from abroad. Young Muslims are permitted to study abroad in Cairo and other Islamic capitals. Bosnian Muslims do not consider themselves anti-Western but rather as an enlightened and progressive outpost of Islam. Nevertheless, Bosnian Muslim publications have applauded the upsurge of Islam in recent years.

Christianity

Christianity, whether Orthodox, Roman Catholic, or Protestant, was shared by the developed and developing countries of yesteryear. Such scholars as Max Weber's *Protestant Ethic and the Spirit of Capitalism*, R. H. Tawney's *Religion and the Rise of Capitalism*, D. McClelland's *The Achieving Society*, and others have discussed the impact of Christianity on economic development. The point is that religion is important because the influence of religious tradition is so enduring. Through its effects on values, attitudes, and incentives, religion influences the economy.

Values and Attitudes

Values and attitudes toward wealth and material gain so crucial if a country's economy is to develop are not universally shared over the world. Indeed Gunnar Myrdal in *Asian Drama* observes that

> the modernization ideals are all in a sense alien to the region [Asia] since they stem from foreign influences. But they have cause to be indigenous in the sense that they have been adopted and shaped by the intellectual elite, who, in turn, have endeavored to diffuse them throughout the population. The other valuations held by the mass of people, and in large part also by the intellectual elite, are mainly "traditional": they use part of an inherited culture long identified with a stagnating society. Related to this is another distinction. While the modernization ideals, both individually and as a system of valuations, are dynamic and interventionist, requiring changes through public policy, all traditional valuations, including those on the most intellectualized level, are static. Even when they are of such a nature as to lend support to the modernization ideals, they themselves are not the driving force. The static character of the traditional valuations is obvious when they appear as inhibitions and obstacles.[22]

One can reasonably ask whether planners and the intellectual elite have a right to impose their values and attitudes on a developing country as a whole. It is not at all clear that in some Third World countries a consensus on modernization exists. Such a consensus may well not exist. There may well be a preference for stability, tradition, and conservatism purchased at the expense of modernization, economic development, and economic nationalism.

Islam, for instance, contains elements that strongly oppose change. Muhammed is supposed to have said that "all innovation is the work of the devil." Unless the *ulama* who interpret the Koran are favorable to change and development, they may, and have, resorted to fanatical opposition up to and including assassination of would-be reformers. This has happened in the case of the Muslim Brotherhood in Iran and Egypt.[23] It continues to be a problem in Islamic countries as witness again Iran in the 1970s and the overthrow of the shah, who apparently attempted to modernize the country without the blessing and support of Iran's *ulama*.

All these personal and social risks are in addition to those normally associated with innovation and change. Little wonder that entrepreneurial spirit is in short supply in these lands. Such attitudes stand in striking contrast to those of Europeans who had taken upon themselves the colonization and development burdens of the new world. The fatalism so widespread in many Third World countries simply serves to reinforce attitudes against science, technology, indeed even against the scientific method of discovery and problem solving.

This does not mean, of course, that change and development in the Third World are impossible. Economic development need not follow the path of developed countries. Other paths are possible. It does mean that a consensus in those countries regarding development must be reached. It also means that if an evolutionary rather than revolutionary path is chosen it is necessary to carefully identify those forces serving as impediments to change. Too often change and innovation are attempted before the groundwork is complete, with predictably disastrous results, for example, Iran. Technical change is likely to be accepted more quickly than, for instance, social or political, although here, too, we should keep in mind Nehru's observation that "you can't get hold of a modern tool and have an ancient mind. It won't work."

A successful model of change incorporating a traditional society to the needs of a modern industrial country is Japan and the Meiji period beginning in the late 1860s. The traditional values of Japanese society such as the family system and the emperor system served as both the motivation for modernization and justification of sacrifices necessary for social change. Everything undertaken was justified as necessary and in loyal service to the emperor and to one's family. The large industrial organizations, or Zaibatsu, that subsequently developed in Japan rested in good measure on these shared traditional values anchored firmly in the past that served the country well in its transformation and development into a modern industrial country.

Another element with which the developing countries of yesteryear were not concerned is unionism and unions. In Third World developing countries, unions are not simply concerned with higher material standards of living but also with political and social issues. In many of these countries unions are, for good or bad, politicized. Some even served as rallying organizations in the struggle for independence. Reluctance to tolerate other sources of power has also resulted in the fact that unions in some developing countries are little more than an arm of government. At times, too, unions in the Third World tend to push for welfare and social programs that some developing countries can ill afford materially.

Education and Technology

Education and technology are considered by many economists as prime movers in the course of economic development. They are factors in raising productivity and so are a more efficient and effective use of available resources. Along with traditional factor inputs of land, labor, and capital we include education and technology, though they are obviously interrelated, especially with such factors as capital. It is also obvious that land and the natural resources that it represents contribute little to economic growth without the application of appropriate technology. This in turn depends on the education of labor in order to increase its capacity to understand and apply technology, which in turn is made possible by the availability of capital. This is, in effect, the well-known interrelationship between labor, land, capital, education, and technology that plays a vital role in promoting a country's economic growth and development.

The application of modern technology and education in an economy has consequences that are seldom fully appreciated by countries in a hurry to develop. For instance, technological change by introducing new methods of production typically requires changes in factor inputs by various industries. As a result, burdens of adjustment may fall unevenly on various factors and sectors of the economy. The country may well find itself undergoing the painful process of structural adjustment, which may have serious political consequences. For instance, not all sectors and segments of the economy and society may be prepared to accept the necessary adjustment. There is, after all, the natural human instinct to protect oneself and more especially one's way of life. Intuitively and quite correctly people feel that a change in economic circumstances may protend a change in society. Indeed it is when society is stepping from one economic structure to another that a crisis is most likely to occur.

It is well known that a great variety of cultural forms are found under any given set of technological and educational conditions. It is also well known that technology and education can, and usually do, interact and serve as powerful influences on a society's culture by providing it with new possibilities and capabilities. Such interaction will very likely require further cultural changes in much the same way as when a stone is dropped into a pool of water.

Education and technology serve a country's standing in international trade by influencing its comparative trade and production advantages. Technological advances in developed countries, especially with regard to new synthetic fibers, for instance, have had the effect of slowing down the demand for some primary products of Third World countries. Thus it is that a country's comparative advantage and trade position may be critically dependent in technological and educational conditions.

The Third World's technological and educational condition has been variously deplored in discussions of "technological dependence," "technological gap," and "brain drain." Countries fear technological dependence will deprive them of economic development and military and political influence. Such dependence, they worry, will serve only to stunt the development of their domestic managerial and technological capabilities. Usually multinational corporations are criticized for their tendency to concentrate research and development activities and high-technology manufacturing in a few parent countries and relegate only unskilled or low value-added operations to their foreign subsidiaries. A consequence may be to retard technological and other skills in the host countries. Developed countries also tend to worry about becoming satellite "branch plant" economies.

A related issue in the Third World and between countries is the technological gap, which is usually taken to mean the production of technology in two or more countries and/or differentials in the usage of technology. It can be argued that no "gap" as such really exists, only a lag between countries (either developed or developing) and industries. The international transfer and diffusion of knowledge and technology serve to close such gaps between countries and industries.

The so-called brain drain is related to the above issues. It is a name assigned to the migration of highly trained people such as engineers, scientists, and other professionals from Third World developing countries to developed countries. Better scientific facilities and all-around opportunities serve to attract such talented people to developed countries. Indeed, it is not always clear that the movement of human capital always has adverse effects on the country losing such capital. For instance, the talented person may not have the opportunity to fully develop and contribute his talents in his country of birth. As a result the world as a whole could be the loser.

Laws

A country's written and unwritten laws and legal framework are an important aspect of its culture, and they are an important factor in promoting or retarding its development. In many respects it is through a country's laws that useful insights may be gained into its attitudes, culture, and religion. The legal systems in the world include civil law, common law, Muslim law, indigenous (tribal, nonliterate) law, as well as variations of these systems. Moreover, in no two countries are laws or the legal framework identical. Countries sharing similar cultural antecedents may tend to be similar. For instance, Muslim countries share similar laws as do many socialist countries and Christian countries. In the Third World, many countries share similar French and British colonial backgrounds. The Koran, as we discussed, provides Islamic countries with a common legal element. So, too, did the Roman Empire influence the legal code of many European and non-European countries.

International law and regional law serve to reduce differences between national laws and the way countries treat legal issues.[24] In a sense, international law does often serve to settle intercultural conflict and assists in adjustment between nations. All of this supposes, of course, that countries are in general agreement about issues they wish to resolve. Current international law includes, in addition to political and military agreements, international investment, trade, labor and other commercial agreements, patents, taxes, and many other areas such as the United Nations, the International Monetary Fund, as well as certain issues dealing with human rights (for example, the European Convention on Human Rights).

The Third World countries, as we discussed, have added their input into the development of international law, particularly in the 1974 "Charter of the Economic Rights and Duties of States." Regional groupings such as the European Economic Community and others have provided additional stimuli to international law development, especially in economic matters. Growth of multinational corporations has encouraged development and extension of international law. Although international law as a body of laws is small compared to national law, it is developing and growing as more nations find it in their interests to participate in the world community. Witness, for example, the UN efforts toward a global commercial code.

The fact is that the Third World countries, many non-Western and often excolonial, are emerging, often with a very different sociocultural and political orientation and with a different set of political and economic problems vis-a-vis the rest of the world. That these Third World nations are attempting to develop by drawing on an outdated Euro-American model of nationalism may well be the most serious obstacle to their rapid and successful development. They are indeed confronted with formidable economic and cultural constraints.

NOTES

1. See, for example, Diego Cordovez, "The Making of UNCTAD: Institutional Background and Legislative History," *Journal of World Trade Law*, May-June 1967, pp. 253-54.

2. See, for example, Branislav Gosović, *UNCTAD, Conflict and Compromise: The Third World's Quest for an Equitable World Economic Order Through The United Nations* (Leiden: A. W. Sijthoff, 1972).

3. George Macesich, *The International Monetary Economy and The Third World* (New York: Praeger, 1981).

4. Simon Kuznets, *Economic Growth and Structure: Selected Essays* (New York: W. W. Norton, 1965), pp. 177-78.

5. Benjamin Higgins, *Economic Development Past and Present* (New York: W. W. Norton, 1968).

6. See, for example, ibid., p. 197; A. E. Kahn, *Great Britain in the World Economy* (New York: Columbia University Press, 1946); A. K. Cairncross, *Home and Foreign Investment, 1870-1913* (Cambridge: Cambridge University Press, 1953), p. 3.

7. Leland B. Yeager, *International Monetary Relations* (New York: Harper and Row, 1966), p. 256, places these estimates for 1955 at around $300 to $400 billion.

8. Yeager (in ibid.) reports that these estimates are from the statement of John H. Adler, citing A. K. Cairncross, in *Foreign Economic Policy*, Hearings before the Subcommittee on Foreign Economic Policy of the Joint Committee on Economic Report (Washington, D.C.: U.S. Government Printing Office, 1955), pp. 453, 463.

9. Higgins, *Economic Development*, p. 198.

10. Ibid., pp. 198-200.

11. See, for example, Louis Schneider and Charles Bonjean, eds., *The Idea of Culture in the Social Sciences* (Cambridge: Cambridge University Press, 1973).

12. Arthur S. Banks and Robert B. Textor, *A Cross-Policy Survey* (Cambridge, Mass.: MIT Press, 1963), pp. 72-75.

13. See, for example, Karl Deutsch, *Nationalism and Social Communication* (Cambridge, Mass.: MIT Press, 1953).

14. For a case study of India, see B. R. Nayar, *National Communication and Language Policy in India* (New York: Praeger, 1969).

15. Leaders of many developing Third World countries who promptly establish an "academy" for the purification and preservation of a favored language should take cognizance of Dr. Samuel Johnson's views 200 years ago in establishing an English Academy patterned after the French Academy. Dr. Johnson blasted

the idea as foolish and unattainable. The result has been that English is perhaps the most "polluted" and "impure" of all languages, borrowing and incorporating from all corners and countries. Unlike French, English has a vitality to achieve and maintain preeminence among world languages. For an interesting discussion of these and related issues, see "Legislating Languages: Will It Work?" *Wall Street Journal*, March 13, 1973, p. 13.

16. See Vern Terpstra, *The Cultural Environment of International Business* (Cincinnati: South-Western Publishing Co., 1978), pp. 56-57.

17. Ibid., pp. 33-37.

18. Robert Slater, *World Religions and World Community* (New York: Columbia University Press, 1968).

19. Gunnar Myrdal, *Asian Drama: An Inquiry into the Poverty of Nations* (New York: Twentieth Century Fund, 1968) discusses, among other issues, the role of cattle in the Indian economy and the largely negative role of the prohibition against their slaughter as one among many other obstructions in the economy. Most writers, including Max Weber, generally conclude that Hinduism has, by and large, a negative effect on the economy.

20. D. K. Rangnekar, *Poverty and Capital Development in India: Contemporary Investment Patterns, Problems, and Planning* (London: Oxford University Press, 1958), p. 81.

21. For a study of the impact of Buddhism on economic development, see Robert C. Lester, *Theravada Buddhism in Southeast Asia* (Ann Arbor: University of Michigan Press, 1972).

22. Myrdal, *Asian Drama*, p. 73.

23. For a useful discussion, see Vera M. Dean, *The Nature of the Non-Western World* (New York: Mentor Books, 1956).

24. See, for example, Branimir M. Janković, *Medjunarodno jano pravo* (International Public Law) (Belgrade: Naucna Knjiga, 1970).

7

THE ECONOMIC ORGANIZATION:
HOW EFFECTIVE?

ECONOMIC ORGANIZATION

Particularly relevant for the emerging nations of the Third World is a long-standing view in economics that product and factor markets, and indeed firms, operate more effectively and efficiently in the core than on the periphery of economic development.[1] Consisting of three parts, this view attempts to explain locational divergencies in economic development.

First, economic development occurs in a specified locational matrix; there may be more than one such matrix in a particular economy or in the world economy. This means that the process of economic development need not occur in the same way, at the same time, or at the same rate in different locations.

Second, these locational matrixes are primarily industrial urban rather than rural in composition.

Third, the existing economic organization works best at or near the center of a particular matrix of economic development, and it works best in those peripheral areas that are favorably situated to such a center. Economic history strongly supports the first two parts, but there is probably disagreement about the third.

One implication of the third proposition is that we should expect to find important differences in the economic organization between core countries and peripheral countries. Another implication is that peripheral countries especially must deal with improving the effectiveness and efficiency of their economic organization. For the most part this is a domestic task. These countries, many in debt, cannot, in essence, wait for such organizations as the International Monetary Fund (IMF) to carry out the task.[2] Politically expedient though it may be to wait for the IMF to do so, the IMF may also impose inappropriate reforms and measures on the domestic economic organization totally at variance with the country's desired economic and sociopolitical institutions. The net effect may well be counterproductive to the intended reforms.

CORE AND PERIPHERAL NATION-STATES: ILLUSTRATIVE EXAMPLES

Europe constitutes a center of a matrix of economic development. It is primarily industrial and urban rather than rural. Its peripheral areas include a number of nations not as highly developed as those in the core. Most of these are comparatively small nations, highly dependent on foreign trade. Their experience is useful for the insights they provide to the emerging nations of the Third World that are similarly situated on the peripheries of development. It is noteworthy that many of the policies in place in these countries are interventionist and nationalist. They do not appear to be singularly successful in promoting a practicing country's overall interests, though there may well be exceptions.

Finland, for instance, is located on the European core's periphery. The country's foreign trade accounts for about one-quarter of its GNP and exports are focused on a few specialized industrial products. The government is very active in promoting, perhaps inadvertently, "creeping mercantilism" by attempting to shore up perceived structural weaknesses in the country's trade. Besides the usual investments in infrastructure, export promotion, subsidies to private industries, and related items, the government has taken part in production directly, amounting to more than the average (10-15 percent) in other OECD countries. In addition to primary production, the government also takes part in key sectors of manufacturing, petroleum refining, chemical and electrical engineering, and heavy metal manufacturing, as well as the pulp and paper industry.

Finland takes the view that in a dependent specialized economy located on a periphery of development the government must intervene directly into the economy in order to create preconditions for sectoral diversification of industrial production and to lessen external industrial and trade dependence. The extensive public enterprises are, however, more a result of ad hoc decisions than of a comprehensive and over-all program of structural changes.

The country's rapid postwar industrial growth has been unstable and vulnerable. The reasonably high level of welfare is quite unevenly distributed socially and regionally. The structural diversification in terms of industrialization has been one sided, including high sectoral concentration with little multiplier effect and a low level of R & D efforts. According to domestic observers this dependent one-sided industrialization ultimately has caused balance-of-payments problems, increasing foreign indebtedness, a high inflation rate, and severe imbalances in the labor market as well as extensive growth in the tertiary sector.[3] In effect, the position in the division of labor of peripheral Finland has, on the one hand, paved the way for industrialization and economic growth and, on the other hand, caused severe structural imbalances and distortion in the country's economic development.[4] Certainly the state is a very important factor in the country's economic affairs.

Consider now peripheral Yugoslavia. The government is again an important factor in economic affairs. According to some observers the country's postwar record is also mixed.[5] One critic (John Moore) finds that the country's industrial growth over the postwar period was unexceptional by world standards. The Republic of Korea and Japan did better, with Israel, Mexico, and Venezuela in the same general range as Yugoslavia. The Soviet Union and the East European countries did about as well as Yugoslavia according to Moore.

Yugoslavia's regional development policy is pronounced a failure and probably is responsible for retarding the country's overall growth —though as Moore notes this may be difficult to substantiate. Gaps in per capita national income among regions widened during the period. The policy failed to stimulate rapid increases in industrial development. In general there was poor performance in the less-developed regions despite the fact that investment as a share of national income was higher in the less-developed regions than elsewhere. The list can go on.

So what went wrong? According to Moore one limiting factor appears to be the system of property rights under self-management, which directly constrained industrialization. Moreover, the system also imposed indirect restraints on the country's development, especially through the agricultural sector, where the bulk of landholdings are private.

It is possible that Moore overstates his arguments. The Yugoslav economy did pretty well for the first 25 years under worker self-management. Certainly it did better than when it was under direct government control. Yugoslav policies and practices were not conceived in a vacuum; and policymakers are receptive to ideas (even "wrong" ideas). Neither the adherents nor the critics of the Yugoslav model are totally wrong. They do, however, miss a great deal of atmosphere and actuality of the Yugoslav scene by concentrating on the country's worker management structure alone. The informal, the intangible, and the personal aspects of the relations between the different groups in Yugoslav society all too easily slip through the economists' and statisticians' fingers. It is in this tricky area that one needs to know more.

The chief problem in Yugoslavia is not one of achieving rapid economic growth; rather it is one of efficiently employing labor and capital resources in the growth process and of controlling growth-related inflationary and balance-of-payments pressures. Many more problems remain to be resolved. Some of them arise out of the rapid transition from a backward agrarian economy to that of a complex industrial one. Other problems are the inevitable results of past mistakes and of a political monopoly exercised by a one-party system. The Yugoslavs are aware of these problems and they have grappled with them, if not always successfully.

Yugoslavia is being rapidly, if haltingly, transformed into an industrial society. It is the first country that has tried the Soviet economic model and that, finding this model unsuitable for its purposes, has decided to go it alone and develop its own unique model. The period of centralized planning and control and the subsequent period of decentralization have convinced many Yugoslavs of the efficiency of the latter way of organizing economic activity. This does not mean that there has been anything like a flight to the market. It does mean that the market is being used as the arbiter of economic problems as indeed it must if the worker managers are to function properly.

The country's experience provides valuable lessons to others that desire to take a short cut to economic development by the imposition of strong central controls. The principal source of economic progress may well be in the seeming chaos that orthodox planners find so repugnant: Human energy, both physical and especially mental, in combination with tools and natural resources are the producers of material progress. Productivity, however, is the singular problem. Human energy here is the key to the problem and it cannot be harnessed as easily as so many kilowatts of hydroelectric power or tons of steel. It must be permitted free play and experimentation in all endeavors if maximum productivity from tools is to be realized.

One important question then concerns the success or failure with which the authorities will be able to cope with the country's problems: How much scope will be permitted to market forces in the formation of relative prices (including incomes). The rapid rise in prices has prompted the authorities to impose all sorts of price ceilings and controls. However justified by the authorities, controls once imposed have a life of their own. They serve simply to compound the existing distortions in the country's price system. Moreover, they subvert the decisions of the worker-managers, thereby undermining the very foundation of the Yugoslav model. It is simply incorrect to argue that the free formation of prices has failed since the reforms of 1965; the evidence is that such formation has not been given a reasonable chance to work. An equally important issue is providing a stable and suitable monetary and financial framework capable of serving the unique Yugoslav model.

Yugoslavia's southern neighbor Greece, considered also a peripheral country, appears to have suffered from a series of injections of statism into an already sick economy by the country's socialist government. For example, Greece's Ministry of Commerce, before any court decision, imposed a $77 million fine on a leading profitable steelmaker.[6] This was twice the company's total capital and, according to reports, is based on dubious charges of illegal export of currency. The minister of commerce is also empowered to close down, by imposing heavy fines, any private company that deviates from the government's price guidelines. The result is that as bankruptcies multiply, unemployment has increased to about 10 percent in 1984, up from 3 percent in 1981. Inflation registered about 20 percent in 1984, which is far above the average for 24 countries in OECD.

The government deficit is increasing and private investment is nonexistent. Indeed, some economists argue that Greece is really in the midst of a process of deindustrialization. In light of the disastrous repercussions of the ruling Socialist Party's statism, the opposition parties and many economists are calling for a drastic limit on state influence, freeing the economy, and encouraging initiative, responsibility, choice, and greater freedom in all areas. The government's political opposition parties, however, have not been able to articulate their concerns in a meaningful manner.

It is noteworthy that China, on the periphery of another core of development, is busy injecting more and more private initiative and incentive into its moribund economy. In the city of Chonghing in Sichuan province reforms are under way to increase competition by increasing enterprises' antonomy and by allowing some large privately owned companies.[7] Evidence suggests that the experiment is indeed succeeding. Thus industrial and agricultural production jumped in 1983 by 11 percent over 1982. According to official Chinese sources the changes have significantly improved local living conditions.

The city also has an industrial trade center that is allowed to by-pass the bureaucratic red tape that normally slows commerce in China. Retailers elsewhere obtain goods from state-run shops, whose inventory has to be approved at city, provincial, and national levels. Through the new center, retailers—including private traders—now can buy and sell whatever they want, and prices are freely determined by market conditions. It is not surprising that the center's shelves are filled with such up-to-date items as fashions from Shanghai and Hong Kong.

Other measures include a free labor exchange for professionals and engineers, floating interest rates for the city's enterprises, workers' wages linked to their factories' performance, flexible outside employment for university faculties, and managers are granted freedom to run their factories without interference by supervising administrators.

Another Third World peripheral country is Peru. According to one study, Peru is an economy very short on competition and legal entrepreneurship thanks to state interventionist policies, including discriminatory granting of licenses, bounties, concessions, and other monopolistic privileges.[8] The country has managed to accumulate regulations restricting economic activity at an average rate of 30,000 per year since 1950. Such regulations, among other things, discourage investment in labor-intensive techniques that reflect local relative scarcities and encourage those that are capital intensive.

The report goes on to state that the country's enormous informal sector, the rigid social structures, the discriminatory use of law to favor the privileged, the subjugation of the Andean population, the restrictions on economic opportunities, and the lack of competition are the consequences of its pattern of regulation. It is thus imperative to the country that the discriminatory barriers to the legal economy are removed and the informal sector is fully integrated into its total economy.

Some idea of the issues is provided in the recommendations of the report by the Institute for Liberty and Democracy to the Peruvian government:

The regulations we seek to eliminate impose massive inefficiencies and have perverse distributional effects—enriching the powerful and the corrupt at the expense of the poor. At present the urban informal sector lacks the following: access to organized credit markets; property rights (only 10 percent of their urban property is backed up by secure titles); publicly supplied enforcement mechanisms to ensure contractual compliance; business organizations, including those conferring limited liability; and a torts system to correct negative externalities and settle disputes. Our program is to reform the current legal system so that it provides the security essential for the expression of entrepreneurship. Only then can economies of scale be realized and resources put to their highest valued use. . . .[9]

In its sixth World Development Report the World Bank examines the way developing countries control prices, including interest rates, exchanges rates, wages, as well as many others.[10] In one sample of developing countries the World Bank finds that prices in the 1970s were controlled least in Malawi, most in Ghana, with a wide range in between. The bank used its index of price distortions to estimate what each country's growth actually was and then compared that with what actually happened. The study shows that growth depends on many things—for example, resources, political stability—apart from price distortion. Nevertheless, price distortion could explain about one-third of the variation in growth among countries. As the Bank succinctly puts it, "prices do matter for growth."

The more far-sighted governments should and do take the evidence seriously. They understand that it is entrepreneurial skill and human capital rather than politicians and bureaucrats that are the mainsprings of development. Moreover, it is extremely difficult to dismantle official controls over the economy once they are established.

Opposition to the price system and markets is certainly not in the interest of Third World countries. They and the world can ill afford bureaucratic tampering with the delicate market mechanism, if we are to judge from the results produced by vast bureaucratic networks of controls and regulation. The issue and principal problem is that control of world inflation and greater reliance on the market mechanism would indeed constitute a "new international economic order." This by no means makes light of the problem of poverty in the Third World. On the contrary, the problem is far too important to be left to decisions of politicians and international bureaucrats, however well intentioned they may be.

Thus the evidence suggests that an important barrier to material progress in emerging countries is the extensive economic controls imposed by government. Indeed, one study by Peter Bauer argues that foreign aid and development planning have thoroughly politicized economic life.[11] Thanks to the West's two main exports to poor countries—foreign aid and development planning—Third World governments have acquired the resources and rationale to deny economic freedom to their subjects. On this view the West is indeed responsible for Third World poverty but not for the usual reasons of neocolonialism and exploitation. The West is culpable because it unleashed the pestilence of development planning, which has crowded out individual initiative and smothered entrepreneurial talent.

Bauer's study underscores examples of rapid economic advance prior to the advent of marketing boards and other government intrusions that confiscated the monies of producers, distorted prices, and suppressed trade. The detailed monopolization by government of the economy means that the acquisition and exercise of political power is all important. It is not only the economic but even the physical survival of large numbers of people who have come to depend on political and administrative decisions.

In the final analysis foreign aid, according to the study, does in fact serve the interests of well-organized lobby groups. The principal groups benefiting from such aid are Western exporters, followed by consultants and the international bureaucracies.

CORE, PERIPHERY, AND THE THEORY OF DEPENDENCY

Policymakers in many Third World countries apparently view material sovereignty and international redistribution as the major policy goals. These goals are to be achieved through the increase of power and prestige of the UN General Assembly and particularly of UNCTAD. The more radical perception of the international economy sets the tone and language for much of the dialogue between Third World countries and the rest of the world.

Ideas underpinning these arguments are derived from the theory of dependency.[12] The theory argues that even though political independence has been gained by Third World countries, the international economic system is a hierarchical power structure in which capitalist countries constitute a center, or metropole, that dominates the developing countries comprising the periphery. The principal element in the theory is that underdevelopment is caused by the international economic system. Moreover, a new form of dependency is being thrust upon Third World countries by multinational corporations operating from the center.

As we have noted, it is possible to distinguish within Europe and other regions of the world a network of core-periphery relations determined by uneven regional development and inequitable division of labor. There is a highly developed core surrounded by a relatively underdeveloped periphery: Yugoslavia, part of Italy, Greece, Spain, Portugal, Ireland, and Finland. This division is characterized partly by differences in living conditions, but it is based on the differences in the conditions of production and external relations. The development of the periphery is conditioned by the development of the core.

The dependency approach that originated in Latin America in the 1960s has been considered useful in offering new insights into analyzing problems of the Third World. It has also been applied in the European context. Thus in the peripheral countries the production structure is one-sided and oriented toward traditional sectors. Growth processes are extensively determined and heavily dependent on exports and imports. Export structure is undiversified and concentrated on resource-based products and traditional manufactures. Potential industrial development is dependent on foreign inputs of capital goods and equipment, technology, know-how, and finance. As a result there is an endemic trade deficit, increasing external debt, price instability, extreme sensitivity to cyclical changes in the world market, low productivity and relatively low wages, structural unemployment, and, finally, emigration. As we have noted, these characteristics are descriptive of the economies of the peripheral European countries.

Small European states such as Austria, Switzerland, the Netherlands, Sweden, and the other countries with a high degree of internationalization in the world's capital and finance markets represent core countries. They are neither peripheral nor developing. Thus small states exist on both sides of the barricade.

There is reason to believe, moreover, that dependence advocates and others who call for a New International Economic Order really and understandably call for a change in the "rules of the game" to facilitate entrance into world markets on the part of those countries of the Third World with growing industrial power and capacity to absorb technology and capital. These countries, sometimes viewed as being on the "semiperiphery," do not envision wrecking the international economic system; indeed, they plan to benefit from it once they have entered the market and gained a greater share. The theory of oligopoly is better able to rationalize such behavior than a competitive model. Some of these new oligopolists in the Third World already have set out to establish their own multinational firms, with a view to sharing oligopoly profits and rents and participating in "managing" the international economic system rather than in wrecking it.

In fact, multinationals from the Third World now rank among the fastest growing enterprises anywhere. Of the 500 largest international companies, 34 are joint ventures with companies in developed countries.[13] Such countries as South Korea, Singapore, Taiwan, Brazil, Mexico, and Yugoslavia lead the drive into multinationals. Indeed, Mexico, Brazil, and India are in the forefront in revising the international patent and trademark system that was established by the dominant core countries to protect, by legal means, their technological monopoly.

THE ISSUE AND CONCEPT OF COMPETITION

Critical to the effectiveness of an economic organization is the issue of competition. In fact, many countries attempt to maintain internal domestic competition as a matter of economic policy. None of this precludes a nation-state from pushing restrictive and interventionist mercantilist policies in the name of "competition." This is made easier since the concept of competition itself is surrounded by controversy and confusion of thought.

Competition takes many forms and thus there are many definitions of it. Its principal forms discussed in economic theory are pure competition, perfect competition, imperfect competition, monopolitic competition, and oligopoly.[14] Useful though they are for theoretical analysis, these concepts do not all directly serve the requirements of policy.

For theoretical work, many economists prefer "perfect competition" and for policy purposes "workable competition."[15]

In essence sellers of closely similar products are numerous enough that no one person and no group dominates a market, and there is freedom of entry to the industry. Given active rivalry among sellers, these conditions assure consumers of an effective range of choices. Some economists also stress standards of performance of an industry as tests of workability or effectiveness of the competition prevailing in it. Most economists also stress that in judging competition in an industry, both its structure and its performance are important sets of criteria.

Competition provides for a better use of resources and insures freedom of choice for consumers and freedom of opportunities for producers. It stimulates economic growth through its encouragement of incentives. It is, moreover, an essential ingredient of a free society. Thus competition is a means to several important ends of both economic policy and public policy in many countries.

There is considerable disagreement as to the actual extent of competition in the world economy. Some economists and other experts argue that competition has been on the decline during the twentieth century, particularly since World War I. On the other hand there is little empirical evidence to substantiate such an allegation. To be sure, some sectors of the world's economy have become more competitive while others have become less so.

Indeed, if it is assumed that competition neither approximates world reality nor can be sustained, what then are the alternatives? Those advocating "new mercantilist" ideas have their own agenda, which we have noted. Other alternatives come readily to mind. They are countervailing power, direct regulation, regulation through codes, and various forms of government ownership.[16] Each of these has serious flaws as a general substitute for competition, both conceptually and as an approximation to world circumstances to which countries must accommodate and adopt.

In general, we no longer have world industries dominated exclusively by a single country; nor isolated local national markets dominated exclusively by local monopolists. Alternatives to the world's consumers, including business firms, have increased, not decreased. The progress of science and technology, the decline in transportation costs, the internationalization of capital and financial markets, and the development of new forms of production and distribution have been both a result and a cause of competition and in fact many countries have attempted to provide competition with a favorable climate. These factors and others have made the world's economy increasingly interdependent and competitive.[17]

There are, of course, disadvantages to competition as critics are quick to point out. They do exist and should neither be ignored nor overlooked. These are the presumed wastes of competition, including the wastes of competitive advertising, of the misdirection of production, of the destruction of natural resources. To be sure there has been much "waste" in the world's economy and competition may have been one of the causes. The important issue, however, is how to sort out the causes of "waste" in the several senses in which that word can be used. Indeed, some of the wastes attributed to competition can be better placed at the door of monopolistic elements intermixed with competition.[18]

Critics of competition seldom fail to attribute to it the cultivation of ignoble and less-desirable patterns of human behavior. In a competitive environment, so the argument goes, people live by their wits, engage in sharp practices, and develop the arts of knavery and trickery. There may even be something to this argument; the open and implied contrast is with the probity and fair dealing of an idealized bureaucracy. Few people who have dealt with actual bureaucracies will deny, however, that they exhibit their own species of double-dealing and guile. Indeed, a good case can be made to show that a commercial society begets honesty among men.[19]

Another criticism directed at competition by its critics is that it does not serve to promote economic stability. Few economists will argue that a competitive economy is perfectly stable. It is, however, less unstable than an economy marked by the rigidities of widespread monopoly. A stable monetary framework, moreover, is an essential component in a competitive national and world economy if the experiences of the 1930s and 1970s are to be avoided.[20]

NATURE AND ROLE OF THE FIRM

Central to the effectiveness and efficiency of a country's economic organization is the firm. The firm itself reflects the country's economic, political, and sociocultural system.

In terms of size and type of organization, firms range from the part-time, one-person operation to the multiproduct, multidivisional, multinational corporation. It is this diversity and heterogeneity on the part of the firm that often obscures its basic role in the economy. At times the firm is conceptualized as a "system of relationship with its role to monitor team production";[21] and at other times as a system for collective action.[22] The firm can also be viewed as basically complementary to the market while at times as an alternative way of organizing resources—or on occasion in moves by firms toward vertical integration and disintegration.[23]

Nonetheless, the firm plays a vital role in the price system. Fritz Machlup describes the firm as "a uni-brain, an individual decision-unit that has nothing to do but adjust the output and the prices of one or two imaginary products to very simple imagined changes in data."[24] The firm is a necessary "theoretical link, a mental construct helping to explain how one gets from the cause to the effect" in the same fashion as "the household in price theory is . . . a theoretical link between changes in prices and changes in labor services supplied and consumer goods demanded."[2][5]

To be sure, firms do other things in addition to adjusting prices and outputs. Indeed, Adam Smith's *Wealth of Nations* focuses on how production is organized within the firm. The organization of production in Smith's well-known pin factory is used by him to illustrate, in short, a principal factor in the growth of the wealth of nations. It is not the invisible hand of competition in the market but rather the visible hand of a cost-conscious and profit-oriented entrepenuer who is responsible for the organization of work within Smith's pin factory. Smith's emphasis on the firm has not been given much attention in economics, even though he noted the importance and predicted the growth of large integrated multiplant enterprises.[26] It is true that Smith, having conceptualized the division of labor in terms of the organization of work within the enterprise, subsequently neglected to develop or pursue systematically such a line of analysis.

The U.S. economic system is one that operates without any central management. Production is in large part carried on in organizations, each of which specializes in particular phases of the productive process and each of which is under the direction of a management. Copeland describes it as a system that has no general manager but a large number of functional foremen.[27] Thus he writes:

> Because there are many organizations engaged in the productive process —many business enterprises each of which is a social organization, not merely a single individual—our economy involves the central management function of providing for functional foremen—determining who shall act as foremen, clothing them with authority to act as foremen and imposing on others who participate in the work of any business enterprise the duty to obey its management.[28]

Provision for these "functional foremen" in the U.S. system is made by two institutions: the property system and the wage system. Thus, writes Copeland,

> the form of property involved is the business proprietorship or net worth. From the point of view of the accountant net worth is merely a residual claim to the assets of a business, what is left of the assets after the claims of creditors are satisfied. But the title to a business is much more than this. In the case of a role proprietorship it conveys to the proprietor the right to manage the business and the right to the profits derived from it. In the case of an incorporated enterprise these rights are conveyed to the

corporation as a legal person, which means in effect that the management is vested in the corporation's directors and officers.[29]

Thus the title to a business empowers the "functional foreman" with managerial authority. The wage system, on the other hand,

> imposes on its employees the obligation of subservience . . . in this kind of a social organization the management not only issues orders to the employees but also in any large enterprise it prescribes and administers rules governing their conduct as employees and inflicts penalties for disobedience, among others the penalty of dismissal. It need scarcely be said that making and administering shop rules and inflicting penalties involve quasi-governmental powers; the setting up of a business organization means in fact establishing a kind of industrial government.[30]

In fact, a business organization is a kind of industrial government—a point that is underscored in our study. The firm does reflect the sociopolitical and economic system in which it operates. The worker-managed firm in Yugoslavia, for instance, operates within a system of market socialism. This is reflected in the manner in which worker-managers formulate goals and in general participate in the managerial processes.[31] So too in the centrally planned economies in the Soviet Union and in Eastern Europe the firm reflects its environment in the manner in which it operates.

Similarly in other societies: Thus it is, for example, that many Muslim scholars interpret the Koran as banning fixed interest (though not other forms of return and profit).[32] Interest is held to be an unfair and exploitative use of money, which Islam sees not as a commodity in itself but as God-given wealth to be used to help those in need and to invest to make economies grow in accordance with Islamic laws. According to some Muslim economists, the modern system of economics based on Adam Smith grew as religious faith declined. In their view, modern economics substitutes materiality and accumulation for faith. Interest rates themselves "increase inflation" and help redistribute money from the less well off, who deposit in banks, to those in business. It is for this reason that such institutions as the Habib Bank in Pakistan resemble Western investment and equity banks and finance houses. These institutions take depositors' money into profit and loss accounts and share profits every three, six, or twelve months. They rely on most individual investments returning a profit to offset those that lose.

In essence, the firm, whether a simple unitary operation or a large diversified corporation, reflects its sociocultural, political, legal, and economic environment in which it is a resource converter in a way in which the market cannot be. The firm converts inputs of labor, materials, ideas, government support, capital, and the like into outputs of goods, services, employment, stimulating exercises, markets, and other conditions by those who provide the inputs.[33] Thus economic activity, writes McNulty,

> involves two types of flows: that of resources and materials to the firm, and that of conversions *from* the firm. Both flows are regulated and controlled by the character of the markets in which they take place, but the connecting link between them—the conversion itself—is a non-market activity which can only occur within the firm.[34]

The efficiency with which the conversion takes place—the organizational and managerial efficiency of intrafirm operations—has been designated by Harvey Leibenstein as "X-efficiency."[35] It is conceptually and analytically different from the allocative efficiency generated by competitive markets, the difference between the two types of efficiency being at bottom the difference between the market and the firm as institutions through which resources are channeled for ultimate consumption. Like the institutions in and through which they are generated, allocative efficiency and "X-efficiency" are different but complementary aspects of the economic process.

The firm is the determinant of what attributes a factor, product, or service is to have and thus what is going to be available for the process of exchange, in which costs and prices will be determined. In its role as price adjustor and carrier of information concerning product or service quality it is a necessary and complementary part of market operations. Organization, as Alfred Marshall suggests, can be called the "fourth factor of production," complementing the classical trinity of land, labor, and capital.[36]

NOTES

1. T. W. Schultz, *Economic Organization of Agriculture* (New York: McGraw-Hill, 1953); and George Macesich, *Commerical Banking and Regional Development in the United States, 1950-1960* (Tallahassee: Florida State University, 1965).

2. See George Macesich, *World Banking and Finance*: *Cooperation Versus Conflict* (New York: Praeger, 1984), for a discussion of the developing countries and their debt problems.

3. See, for instance, Kimmo Kiljunen, "Finland in the European Division of Labour," *Small States in Europe and Dependence*, edited by Otuiar Holl (Vienna: Wilhelm Braumuller, Universitats-Verlagsbuchhandlung, December 1983), pp. 145-63.

4. Ibid.

5. A number of studies are readily available for a critical view. See John H. Moore, *Growth with Self-Management: Yugoslavia Industrialization in 1952-1975* (Stanford, Calif.: Hoover Institution Press, 1980). For a more balanced view, see R. Lang, G. Macesich, and D. Vojnic, *Essays on The Political Economy of Yugoslavia* (Zagreb: Informator, 1982).

6. J. C. Loulis, "Greeks Distrust a Party Bearing No Ideas," *Wall Street Journal*, September 5, 1984, p. 33.

7. Victor Fung, "Chonghing: China's Economics Laboratory," *Wall Street Journal*, September 5, 1984, p. 36.

8. Hernando de Soto, "Legacy of Mercantilism Stymies Market Creativity in Peru," *Wall Street Journal*, January 4, 1985, p. 15.

9. Ibid., p. 15.

10. World Bank, *World Development Report* (Washington, D.C.: World Bank, 1983); and Macesich, *World Banking and Finance*.

11. Peter Bauer, *Reality and Rhetoric: Studies in the Economics of Development* (Cambridge, Mass.: Harvard University Press, 1983).

12. See, for example, T. Dos Santos, "The Structure of Dependence," *The American Economic Review*, Papers and Proceedings, May 1, 1970, pp. 231-36; and *Latin America's Political Economy* (Garden City, N.Y.: Anchor Press Books, 1972).

13. See George Macesich, *The International Monetary Economy and the Third World* (New York: Praeger, 1981).

14. See George J. Stigler, "Perfect Competition, Historically Contemplated," in *Essays in the History of Economics*, edited by George J. Stigler (Chicago: University of Chicago Press, 1965), pp. 234-67; and Donald S. Watson, *Economic Policy: Business and Government* (Boston: Houghton Mifflin, 1960), especially Chapter 9. See also Morris A. Copeland, "Institutionalism and Welfare Economics," *American Economic Review*, March 1958, pp. 1-30 (presidential address delivered at the Seventieth Annual Meeting of the American Economic Association, Philadelphia, December 28, 1957). See also Paul J. McNulty, "A Note on the History of Perfect Competition," *Journal of Political Economy*, August 1967, pp. 395-99.

15. J. M. Clark proposed the term "workable competition" for policy purposes. J. M. Clark, "Toward a Concept of Workable Competition," *American Economic Review*, June 1940, pp. 241-56.

16. Watson, *Economic Policy*, Chapter 9.

17. See Macesich, *The International Monetary Economy*.

18. Copeland, "Institutionalism and Welfare Economics," pp. 4-6, notes six important examples of divergences between what is profitable and what is good public policy. These include petroleum and natural gas resources; short-term leases; the individual labor bargain (similar to a short-term lease); de facto torts (situations in which an individual inflicts damage on another person or another person's property or exposes another person having a reasonably adequate remedy at law—for example unsafe buildings, unsanitary arrangements, environmental

pollution); eminent domain; and corporate management, which aims at transferring resources from corporation stockholders to financiers and corporation officers.

19. On the other hand, Copeland (ibid., pp. 12-13), in discussing competition, writes

> And many of those who take the perfect market view would agree with those who take the institutional-supplements view that competition is inadequate as a regulator when it comes to price differentials and other discriminatory practices; for competition frequently means discrimination. In fact, a competitor that gets ahead in an industry may do so in substantial part by developing business connections, i.e., arrangements that give him preferential treatment in terms of financing, in terms of purchase, in access to market information, in the award of private contracts, even in preferential treatment in the administration of public office. The fact that various businessmen who have become public officials seem to have found it difficult to understand our conflict-of-interest laws bears witness to the prevalence of such discriminatory arrangements in the business world. They are not only prevalent; many businessmen seem to think freedom to make such arrangements is an essential feature of our free enterprise system.

20. George Macesich, *The Politics of Monetarism: Its Historical and Institutional Development* (Totowa, N.J.: Rowman and Allanheld, 1984).

21. Armen A. Alchian and Harold Demsetz, "Production, Information Costs and Economic Organization," *American Economic Review*, December 1977.

22. Kenneth J. Arrow, "Towards a Theory of Price Adjustment," in *The Allocation of Economic Resources*, Moses Abramovitz et al. (Stanford, Calif.: Stanford University Press, 1959).

23. Paul J. McNulty, "On the Nature and Theory of Economic Organization: The Role of the Firm Reconsidered," *History of Political Economy*, Summer 1984, pp. 233-53.

24. Fritz Machlup, "Theories of the Firm: Marginalist Behavior," *American Economic Review*, March 1967, p. 9.

25. Ibid.

26. See, for instance, the useful discussion of these issues by McNulty in "On the Nature," pp. 236-38.

27. Copeland, "Institutionalism and Welfare Economics," pp. 13-14.

28. Ibid., p. 13.

29. Ibid., p. 14.

30. Ibid.

31. Lang, Macesich, and Vojnic, *Essays on the Political Economy of Yugoslavia*; George Macesich, *Proceedings and Reports* (Tallahassee: Center for Yugoslav-American Studies, Research and Exchanges, The Florida State University), Volumes 10-17. See also M. Damjanovic and D. Voich, eds., *The Impact of Culture Based Value System on Management Policies and Practices: Yugoslav and United States Issues and Viewpoints* (New York: Praeger, forthcoming).

32. See Macesich, *The International Monetary Economy*, pp. 108-14.

33. McNulty, "On the Nature," p. 251.

34. Ibid., p. 251.

35. Harvey Leibenstein, "Allocative Efficiency vs. X-Efficiency," *American Economic Review*, June 1966, pp. 392-415. See also Paul J. McNulty, "Allocative Efficiency vs. X-Efficiency: A Comment," *American Economic Review*, December 1967, p. 1250.

36. Alfred Marshall, *Principles of Economics* (London: Macmillan, 1930).

8

THE MULTINATIONAL ENTERPRISE:
A CHALLENGE TO
NATIONAL SOVEREIGNTY?

THE ISSUES

The rapid growth of the multinational enterprise is viewed by many observers as a challenge to the nation-state and its sovereignty. This is particularly the case by those advocates of economic nationalism or mercantilism whose concept of the state is that of an entity transcending individual interests. Economic nationalism shares with its original ancestry mercantilism, the protection of domestic industry, and an all-powerful state. The preference is for domestic ownership and control of productive facilities, even though considerable economic inefficiency may result.

Consider now the multinational enterprise. A corporation becomes multinational or transnational when its management begins to plan, organize, and control its multinational production on a worldwide scale. National markets, in effect, become segments of broader regional world markets. For our purposes a multinational or transnational corporation or enterprise is defined as an enterprise that takes part in foreign production through its own affiliates, exercises direct control over the policies of its affiliates, and seeks to follow a worldwide strategy.

In the continuing discussions of multinational enterprises, there tends to be agreement that: first, multinational or transnational enterprises make a significant contribution to world welfare; second, not all partners share the benefits equally if at all (this appears to be the case not only between the host country and the home country but indeed between labor and capital); third, that political, economic, and social considerations all point to the need for companies to adopt policies that are less dominated by the home interests of the home country's organizations. The challenge is, of course, to develop policies that effectively deal with these issues while at the same time allowing multinational corporations to make their contribution to worldwide welfare. In host countries that differ in one or another aspect, depending in part on whether developed or developing, a multinational corporation impacts on the elite, often challenges ideologies, and results in a clash of cultures. In the home countries the multinational corporation often adds to a feeling that control is lost, jurisdictional conflict is increased, and psychic pain at times tends to conceal any benefits derived, especially where sensitive defense issues may be concerned.

For instance, governments as a rule, in the formulation and execution of science policy, channel grants and subsidies to indigenously owned enterprises. This is understandable since governments usually have not been anxious to subsidize the research of U.S.-owned subsidies. Much the same policies, for instance, are followed in Canada, by the Industrial Reorganization Corporation in Great Britain, and by the Institut de Développement Industriel in France. Indeed the disposition of public agencies to favor locally owned producers is being formalized and strengthened in many countries. All of this is consistent in contemporary economic nationalism and its focus on cultivating domestic industry.

SOME MISCONCEPTIONS

The importance of multinational corporations is but another manifestation—albeit an important one—of the changing postwar international economy. These corporations represent an important element in promoting trade and development throughout the postwar world. As such they serve to integrate the international economy and provide access to world markets for many small developing countries in the Third World.

In discussing transnational corporations it is useful to dispel at the outset several misconceptions regarding their role and stance, especially in Third World countries.[1] First, developing countries are not as important to the transnational corporations as is often argued. Except in the case of the extractive mining and oil industry, the bulk of their sales, revenues, profits, and indeed growth are earned in industrial countries. This is particularly true for the world's major manufacturing, distributive, and financial corporations.

Second, more than "resources" from abroad are needed to trigger and sustain economic growth and development in a country. Domestic resources must be energized to have a "multiplier effect." Moreover, the ability of a country to profitably and effectively absorb resources may be quite limited owing to domestic factors.

Third, the transnational corporation by effectively and efficiently integrating and allocating resources on a worldwide scale does so not at the expense of the host country but indeed assists in integrating its host country into the international economy. At the same time the transnational corporation may well provide the host country with bargaining leverage that it otherwise would not have. A policy of self-sufficiency is not possible for even the best endowed country. The integration of the productive capabilities and advantages of integrating developing countries into the international economy is the most sensible approach.

Further, the "parent corporation" seldom, if indeed ever, has 100 percent ownership of a transnational enterprise. There is agreement that 100 percent ownership may be desirable since it is likely to make unity of action planning and other related activities easier, hence the idea of restricting a foreigner to a minority participation. On the other hand, the increasing scarcity of capital may well push transnational enterprises to insist on host country participation in such various forms as joint ventures with local capital and partnerships. The host country may be increasingly reluctant to enter such arrangements, viewing them as drains on already scarce local capital. For all its difficulties, mixed ownership of transnational enterprises may become increasingly favored, especially if world scarcity of capital continues into the future.

THE ECONOMICS OF THE TRANSNATIONAL OR MULTINATIONAL ENTERPRISE

The objectives of a firm are not always clear cut. This is as true for the transnational enterprise as it is for others. Simply asking a firm's managers what their objectives are does not necessarily yield satisfactory results. One soon discovers that managers agree to any plausible objective about which they are asked. Transnational enterprise managers say they wish to maximize their own incomes (pecuniary and nonpecuniary), maximize the firm's profits, maximize the firm's sales, minimize costs, minimize government (domestic and host) intervention, and at the same time increase and develop overseas affiliates. Since it is seldom possible to serve simultaneously a multiplicity of such goals, it is more important to determine what these managers do than what they say they do. Even the most casual observer will discover that they settle on one objective or some compromise among them.

This is simply another way of saying that a transnational enterprise will seek to maximize pecuniary and nonpecuniary profits. An enterprise's decision thus can be analyzed without recourse to a kind of "budget restraint" whose existence distinguishes the traditional analysis of the firm from that of consumers. In fact, existing theories of the firm are able to explain much of the behavior of transnational enterprises.

The problem considered by some analysts as important is that of a transnational corporation composed of a large number of geographically diverse operating units.[2] Thus the corporation may pursue profit maximization while having one affiliate that seems to accept some inefficiency—for instance, to encourage a young management group; another affiliate may attempt to maximize roles at a very low profit goal so as to ensure market share in a market with long-run growth; while a third affiliate in a Third World location is given considerable managerial leeway for political reasons to ensure access to raw materials and minimize risks of confiscation.

Oligopoly

The economics of the transnational enterprise tends to be approached from the viewpoint of oligopoly theory. This theoretical situation is characterized by mutual interdependence among various sellers arising as a result of the smallness of the number of sellers in the particular market area. It is also one of the most complex portions of price theory since oligopoly is not a single clear-cut case. It includes a wide range of related cases, all characterized by mutual interdependence but differing in the exact degree of interdependency and the exact policies followed by the firms.

Oligopoly, in the sense of mutual interdependence, arises whenever the number of firms is sufficiently small so that a price change by any one firm affects the sales of the other firms to such an extent that readjustments are made by these firms. If there are only two or three or eight or nine producers of a product, or major producers, in an industry, oligopoly will obviously exist. Given the complexities and diversities of oligopoly, the analysis is usually broken down into several segments.

Consider, first, complete oligopoly so that relationships among the firms are sufficiently close to permit the maximization of the joint profits of the firms as a group. Such a situation may occur as a result of spontaneous coordination of policies among several firms or from conscious cooperation on the part of managers of the firms.

Maximization of joint profits requires the determination of the price on the basis of the total demand schedule for the product and the summation of the marginal cost curves of the several firms. By collective action in the case of collusion, firms will estimate the demand and cost schedules and set the optimum price and output. If prices are set by one firm and followed by all others, this firm will attempt to price on the basis of the total demand and cost schedules rather than on its own, and other firms will go along with the decision of this firm. In the absence of collusion, maximum joint profits can be obtained only if each firm, acting independently, correctly estimates the price that is the optimum from the group's standpoint on the basis of the firm's estimate of the total demand schedule for the product.

Total profits are shared by the various firms according to relative costs and sales. The firms with the lowest costs and those with large sales volumes will obtain the largest amounts. But this in turn depends on relative consumer preference for the several brands. In the case of collusion among firms, agreed-upon market shares and profit division will likely depend upon the relative bargaining strength of the firms. Such strength, in turn, is likely to depend upon bargaining skill, ability to carry out threats successfully, relative costs, and consumer preference.

The attainment of complete oligopoly is a very difficult task indeed. Firms simply do not surrender their freedom of action easily, especially if they are under pressure to increase their share of the total market in order to increase their profit. It is most unlikely that demand and cost schedules for all firms will be identical or required by the maximum joint-profit price. Such a situation would require closings of higher cost firms and concentration of production in the lower cost firms. The issue, of course, is to select firms that are to close. The result very likely will be to compromise on price. Such a compromise will not be readily accepted by all firms, so there is an incentive to break away from competitive pricing.

Moreover, the problems of estimating the total demand curve will make selection of the optimum price difficult, since various firms very likely will have different views about the optimum. The net result will be that actual selection will depend on bargaining power of the several firms. In addition, optimum profit maximization may depend on other objectives as well. For example, some objectives may include forcing other firms to carry out desired policies, or to drive other firms out of business, or to test bargaining power.

Difficulties in reaching an agreement are also compounded by other factors influencing the attainment of maximum group profits. Failure of firms to agree upon product changes, advertising policies, and introduction of new techniques are cases in point. Each firm is reluctant to come to an agreement when it feels itself confident that it can do better in any or all of these areas than the others. Price changes lead to changes by competitors that a given firm may not be able to meet. There is, as a result, a tendency to more readily reach price agreements. The fact is, however, that profits will eventually be eroded for the oligopoly group through price competition.

Even if agreement among existing firms in an oligopoly group regarding maximum-profit price is forthcoming, there is usually present the fear that such a price may encourage new firms to enter. The existence of "excessive profits" serves as an incentive to new firms, which may overcome such barriers to entry as large capital requirements, established reputations and relationships, and large volume output. The net result is that firms may deliberately hold prices below the optimum short-run, maximum-profit levels. They may prefer so-called lower reasonable profits rather than risk and encourage entrance of new firms.

In addition, difficulties in coordinating the action of several firms in an oligopoly reduce the likelihood of frequent price changes, even in the face of changing circumstances. Conditions and circumstances do change so that even if the price set originally is one yielding maximum joint profit it is unlikely to do so for any length of time.

The net effect is that difficulties in establishing a maximum joint profit for an oligopoly group render such an exercise largely futile, even under the best of cooperative circumstances among firms. The fact is that little mutual interdependence exists among firms, especially as the number increases to bring about a mutually satisfactory price yield and optimum joint profit. These difficulties lead economists to turn to partial oligopoly theory.

Partial oligopoly theory deals with situations in which joint profits of the group are not maximized. Such cases may be "spontaneous co-ordination" on a limited scale rather than agreement among firms. The essential difference between the price setting by oligopolists and that by other firms is the importance of the influence on the firms' demand schedules of possible reaction by competitors. In effect, interdependence will very likely lead to reduced elasticity of the demand schedule of the product of the firm beneath what it would be in the absence of such interdependence.

There is also the tendency to create considerable uncertainty regarding the exact nature of demand schedules facing firms since a firm can seldom be certain about the exact reaction of other firms to a price rise or decrease. A price reduction by one firm may lead to a significant, an insignificant, or no change at all in its sales volume as competitors take appropriate action. For all practical purposes, the firm may now be faced with several demand schedules, depending upon the reaction of other firms. Firms then have an incentive to minimize frequency of price changes and/or resort to techniques of pricing that minimize reaction on the part of other firms.

One means for reducing the degree of uncertainty is simply not to make independent price changes but rather to adopt and follow policies and prices set by other firms. This is the "price leader" situation so typical, some argue, in oligopoly. Thus a leading firm producing a large portion of total output tends to dominate the pricing. Smaller firms are then presumably able to sell as much as they wish at the price established by the leading firm. This is achieved by the large firm setting prices through pricing techniques. Though these techniques are not likely to maximize profits for the firms as a group, they may represent the "best" possible solution. This is consistent with the assumption that firms seek to maximize profits. The essence is that the use of average-cost pricing or cost-plus pricing provides a relatively simply method of price setting and adjustment that minimizes "competitive disturbances," particularly if more or less uniform methods of allocation of common costs to various products are followed.

Under oligopoly conditions, considerable opportunity is provided for the use of product variation, advertising, and other forms of selling activities. Since price tends to stabilize at a given figure and price reductions are dangerous, in order to expand sales and thus lower average cost, they typically turn to other safer forms of selling activities as a means of increasing their sales. Competitors can readily meet price cuts but nonprice competition is more subtle and so more difficult to match, if at all.

Nonetheless, there does appear to exist within oligopoly a feeling of interdependence with respect to selling activities, just as there is with respect to prices. In the case of perfect collusion, for instance, forces may agree and select product and selling policies so that profits for the group are maximized. Again, perfect collusion is seldom, if ever, achieved. Indeed, such scattered evidence as exists suggests that firms are even less likely to agree in a common course on selling and product policies than on a price policy. For reasons discussed above, firms feel on firmer ground in following independent policies with regard to such policies than they do in price changes whereby competitors are very likely to follow suit quietly.

The absence of complete collusion among firms drives them into increasing their selling activities so as to increase their share of the market. Competitors, of course, will follow suit. The net effect very likely will be to cancel out much of the selling activity efforts and none of the firms will gain in sales volume. If firms are aware of interdependence in such activities, they are less likely to engage in them.

As in such other imperfect market situations as monopoly, price discrimination may also be practiced in oligopoly. It will, however, require more imagination to carry out since firms must agree on the prices to be charged in various markets, or independently follow identical price policies. Such cooperation is unlikely so that price discrimination is less likely than under complete monopoly.

Thus far our concern with oligopoly theory has been of the short-run variety. The long-run variety is defined so as to allow an industry to grow or to decline and allows resources to move from one industry to another, for investors and for persons entering the labor force to choose among industries. In many of the big oligopolistic industries, in the long run, technological change occurs and consumer demands shift. New products for consumers come on the market as new machines, new processes, and new materials appear in the production function of firms. In the long run demands are more elastic.

The net effect is that over the long run there is a tendency toward uniform levels of profits in the oligopolistic industries (as indeed in others) to prevail, given the mobility of resources over time. To be sure, the tendency is proximate since some barriers to entry persist. The point is that monopolistic elements in oligopoly seem to become less important in the long run. There is a tendency that the allocation of resources under oligopoly is, by and large, tolerably close to efficiency. There are pressures to reduce costs, and production does appear responsive to consumer demand.

Oligopoly, then, is a form of competition. As a representation of reality this model is certainly not an impossibility. Noncollusive behavior of this kind, based on good if not perfect information, must sometimes occur. We shall consider its empirical importance as it applies to transnational enterprise; but let us consider first a "cartel model," which is usually looked upon as merely a temporary form of oligopoly.

Cartel

A cartel is an explicit agreement, typically informal, among independent firms (or countries) on prices, output, and usually on such other matters as division of geographical sales. Treating of cartels under the heading of oligopoly is accepted by most economists for several reasons. Cartels are usually short term. Firms do have the desire for large joint profits and so the desire to form cartels. Firms are likely, however, to disagree over the division of joint profits. This tendency is a leading factor of the breakup of cartel arrangements.

Analysis of cartel situations is usefully divided into "perfect cartels" and "imperfect cartels." A perfect cartel is an agreement among firms in an industry that results in maximization of joint profits of the member firms. The coordinating organization presumably has full knowledge of the demand for the output of the industry at each possible price. The coordinating organization as a result can calculate marginal revenue for the industry. It also knows the marginal costs of all the firms and can calculate the marginal cost of each volume of output for the industry. The organization then sets marginal revenue equal to marginal cost. This gives the price and output for the industry. The organization allocates to each firm that output at which the firm's marginal cost equals the level of industry marginal cost selected so as to maximize joint profits of the industry.

Imperfect cartels originate in the fact that firms are unwilling to give up all their sovereignty, as would be required under a perfect cartel. They wish to retain their identities and freedom of action. This means that although imperfect cartels can raise prices and profits, they do not reach the levels of monopoly.

In general, after fixing prices a cartel usually must set sales or output quotas. This does not have to be done if industry demand is growing as fast or faster than the expansion of industry output. Typically, however, output quotas have to be set to maintain the cartel price. The method whereby the division of profits is to take place usually leads to conflict. There is incentive to cut price secretly and chisel in every way and means possible since additional sales at covertly negotiated lower prices are profitable.

Other Oligopoly Hypotheses

These are in essence the more important oligopoly theories. It is important to note that there are several hypotheses regarding price and output under oligopoly. The result is that economic theory cannot give much support to economic policy. More useful models of oligopoly would assist considerably in improving the standards of economic regulation. These issues are already highly complex on the domestic scene by government attempts to regulate radio and television broadcasting in metropolitan market areas, air transportation, and the like. Attempts to do so on the international level are even more complex, as I shall discuss below.

The applications of theories of oligopoly to problems of economic policy, however, are very difficult indeed. Lack of a set of agreed-upon models of oligopoly means in effect that economic theory cannot give much support to economic policy. We can only hope that the future will bring advances in the theory of oligopoly that will give a firmer grounding to economic policy directed toward coming to grips with these issues and in applying them in formulating economic policy.

In fact, the models of oligopoly discussed show prices and outputs ranging between monopoly and perfect competition. For oligopoly to have the same price and output as monopoly, the necessary assumptions are uniformity of costs and products, perfect knowledge, no objective other than profit maximization, and either the mutual recognition of uniformity and interdependence or the actions of the perfect cartel. Price leadership, imperfect cartel, and incomplete collusion can give results close to monopoly or perfect competition. They can give prices and output between the extremes. As a result, theory cannot say much that helps in assessing the performance of oligopolistic industries.

As for nonprice competition, there is consensus that quality and advertising can be competitive variables. How nonprice competition affects economic welfare is difficult to say at this point in the development of oligopoly theory.

In summary, the interdependence of firms in oligopoly markets—where a firm's action and the reaction of other firms result in shifting revenue and cost curves for all firms in the market—appears to lead to indeterminate outcomes. By making special restrictive assumptions, oligopoly theorists have been able to build models that yield determinate results, but this has led to nearly as many theories of oligopoly as there are oligopoly theorists. Oligopoly markets are considered by many to be analogous to a poker game, where elements of strategy and bluff play important roles. For this reason, some theorists have attempted to apply the theory of games to the analysis of oligopoly markets, but as yet there have been no satisfactory results.

Concern with oligopoly theory and other monopolistic tendencies raises major questions of public policy toward firms with monopoly power. This concern is typically expressed with transnational enterprises as well, since they are viewed by many people as containing elements of monopoly power. Do product differentiation and advertising waste resources, or do they result in greater welfare in terms of variety of goods on the market? Are oligopoly firms an undesirable locus of economic and political power resulting in misallocation of resources, or is their size necessary to capture all the economies of scale available in a modern technical society? If oligopolies are undesirable, should these firms be reduced in size by international and national antitrust action, or should the size of the firm be left alone and the firms either controlled or owned by the host government? The fact is that economic analysis may not answer these questions to the satisfaction to everyone concerned.

EMPIRICAL EVIDENCE

Such empirical evidence as we have is consistent with the profit-maximizing behavior of transnational corporations.[3] So, too, is evidence suggesting that oligopoly models do provide useful insights into their operations. Admittedly these are bits and pieces of evidence gathered from various sources and by various means, including interview evidence, which is open to various interpretations. Thus growth and profits are often synonymous with profit-maximizing behavior as reported by interview studies. Aharoni's study, on the other hand, does suggest that on occasion transnational corporate behavior is not simply disguised profit maximization.

Expenditures on foreign plant and equipment and the flow of direct investment tend to be attributed to profit-maximizing behavior. Oligopolistic interdependence is also suggested in the "bunching" of entry consistent with U.S. industry concentration indexes and with profitability of investment abroad in the relevant industry. In essence, transnational enterprise behavior can be viewed as a form of constrained profit maximization, where financial, structural, environmental, and general resource variables limit pursuit of maximum profits.

In order to test the view that large oligopolistic industries are out in front in introducing innovation and change, Hood and Young, drawing on J. E. S. Parker's study, present evidence suggesting that there are relatively few research-intensive corporations (17 out of a total of 136) that are not at the same time transnational.[4] Parker's data do suggest statistically significant relationships between the intensity of research and the degree of multinationality.

Moreover, on the sensitive issue of centralization and decentralization of distribution of innovative R & D between parent and affiliate, a good case can be made for either view. Concentrating R & D in the home country reduces problems associated with financial control, costs of communication and policing, and potential divergence from central product policies. Cultural problems and differences of coordinating R & D may also be reduced by centralization.

The case for decentralization of R & D activities and spreading these activities to affiliates abroad includes such reasons as perhaps lower costs in the affiliate country, close links to market, environmental conditions, competitors may be more easily monitored, and scientific and technical advances can be more readily followed. Such evidence as we have, however, suggests that for U.S. transnationals less than 5 percent of R & D spending occurs abroad. Indeed, when R & D spending is related to sales it appears that the rate of expenditure at the affiliate level is only about half the rate of private U.S. R & D.

If we look at only R & D expenditure by large transnational enterprises the innovation picture may well be distorted. For instance, evidence suggests that large firms may be more important in minor improvement inventions and that small firms and independent inventors are the principal sources of basic invention and major breakthroughs. Indeed, these issues merge into the strategies of oligopoly. Each may seek to let the others bear the brunt of risk, experiment, and high initial cost while waiting for the appropriate moment to step in and scoop up the major gains. When each waits for the other to take the first dangerous step, it is perfectly possible that that first step will not be taken at all.

Schumpeter's view—that innovation, change, and high productivity in the economy depend on large firms with extensive oligopoly power to administer price—contrasts with the evidence that frequently the smaller and middle-sized firms are the low-cost producers of an industry. In addition, foreign affiliates along with many plants, factories, shops, and divisions are autonomous operating units and can act as independent agents in the market with no fragmentation of R & D activities. However, Schumpeter's view may well have less to do with the market structure and the organization of production than with the optimum size firm capable of undertaking the transformation costs. These are costs of making a change, not of an operation, but of setting up an operation. An example may serve to illustrate the point. A small peasant farm as a unit of operation may be too small and so incapable of transforming itself into using more advanced production techniques. A transnational enterprise by its very size wields sufficient economic power to undertake the transformation costs necessary to change economic processes.

Pricing practices of transnational enterprises theoretically can be sorted out with help from oligopoly theory. Empirical evidence to support such behavior is scarce. Such scattered quantitative evidence as we have suggests that the "cost-plus" and "negotiated prices" familiar to oligopoly theory are in use with respect to transfer pricing in intrafirm transactions between parent and subsidiaries. These practices may also apply to independent buyers. It is difficult to say how widespread the practice of manipulative transfer pricing is, since managers are reluctant to admit to these practices, which are viewed as outside of market transactions and enable transnational enterprises to evade many of the checks on corporate behavior provided by national laws.

Some idea of the complexity of intrafirm transactions is suggested by its various forms, including: locating profits in an affiliate where the host country taxes are lower (and conversely restricting profits where taxes are higher); withdrawing funds from an affiliate by increasing prices on goods sold to that affiliate by other affiliates or by the parent entity in a transnational enterprise network; and financing an affiliate by reducing prices on goods sold to it by other affiliates or the parent organization. Still other forms are employed, such as juggling the allocation of overhead and joint costs, including R & D, advertising, and overpricing the plant and equipment used to set up or expand a foreign facility.

A transnational enterprise's decision to employ transfer pricing is encouraged by tariff barriers in effect in the importing country, the absolute and relative differences in tax rates among various countries, and host government policies regarding the remittance of profits, difficult labor relations, and currency restrictions. Strictly domestic incentives to employ transfer pricing include varying degrees of ownership of affiliates and a desire to place profits where a firm enjoys the largest ownership position, and using pricing techniques to allocate markets among affiliates.

Third World developing countries face singular difficulties in dealing with the transfer pricing issue of transnational enterprises. The United Nations Group of Eminent Persons studying issues posed by transnational enterprise estimates that more than one-fourth of the value of all international trade is in goods of an intragroup.[5] Additional intraenterprise transactions occur in services, R & D, and administrative functions. The UN group concludes that scope for price manipulation is extensive. Access to meaningful information on the part of authorities in developing countries is at best limited. George Ball has succinctly stated: "Though the host government can insist on seeing the books of the local subsidiary, it cannot examine the books of the parent, and even if it could, it would not have the highly trained manpower to make informed reallocations of earnings and costs."[6] Moreover, in a world of cultural and language barriers, complex products, currency fluctuations, and oligopoly strategies, the ability of transnational enterprise to evade and avoid detection is considerable.

People who argue in favor of the so-called dependency theory allege that transnational enterprises use transfer pricing as one means for controlling the economic potential to the peripheral Third World countries. The extent to which transnational enterprises use transfer pricing is, as noted above, difficult to ascertain empirically. Some people, indeed, argue that various organizational impediments, together with governmental requirements, have rendered the use of transfer pricing well below its potential.

THE ISSUE OF ENTRY AND COMPETITION

In Third World countries and particularly those countries with budding and developing transnational enterprises of their own, the issue of entry and competition into such activity attracts considerable attention. I have discussed elsewhere the growing importance of home-grown transnational enterprises in several of the Third World countries. It may be argued that demands for a New International Economic Order originate in part on the desire of these countries to facilitate entrance and access to markets for their own fledgling transnational enterprises. In short, these countries may be immediately motivated more by self-interest in promoting the case for reducing barriers to entry and increasing competition in transnational enterprises than by a strictly new economic order as such.

The fact is that from the point of view of competition and transnational enterprise, there is little presumption one way or the other. In some instances transnational enterprises have introduced more competition to a host-country market. On the other hand, instances do exist whereby such enterprises, thanks to their size and market power, have reduced competition. As a result it is difficult to strike a balance of competitive effects apart from indicating some direction of competitive and restrictive forces.

Studies suggest that entry of foreign firms into markets dominated by one or a few domestic enterprises may stimulate competition by increasing capacity, leading to a price reduction or at least weakening the possibility of a price increase. One study, for instance, reports that the appearance of U.S. firms in Great Britain resulted in the break-up of virtual or potential monopolies for watches, tires, soaps and detergents, radiators, boilers, clocks, appliances, refrigeration equipment, and excavating machinery.[7] This study also reports that market entry of foreign firms only caused monopoly positions to be replaced by oligopolies with the effect in several instances of holding down price increases and in some instances actually reducing prices further during price declines. In Australia, foreign investors turned a monopoly in tobacco and detergents into an oligopoly with profits in these industries reduced. In France, import substitution by the protection of foreign affiliates led to an improvement in the balance of payments, which then allowed trade policy to be liberalized; trade liberalization in turn increased import competition and reduced prices in the chemical, pharmaceutical, machinery, and electronic sectors as well as other sectors.

Practices of transnational enterprises in restricting competition continue to receive unfavorable attention. Though such practices may not differ from domestic firms, they become increasingly important because transnational enterprises tend to be larger in terms of economic, financial, and technological power at their disposal. The Organization for Economic Cooperation and Development in its report identifies several categories of restrictions as representing major breaches of competition.[8] These include international allocations of production and markets, discriminatory pricing, mergers that decrease competition and increase concentration, and discriminatory patent licensing restrictions.

The dominant issue, however, is entry and the nature of incentives and barriers facing potential entrants into an industry and the consequences of these factors on structure and performance in the industry. On this score insights can be had, as noted, by turning to oligopoly theory. Six factors influence entry into oligopolistic industry;[9] in a very broad sense they are: institutional framework and government policy, performance, economic considerations, economic informational uncertainties, time lags, and strategic behavior of market participants.

The first factor is relatively straightforward. Laws and the domestic and international framework within which competition takes place determine the incentives as well as the disincentives to entry. The second factor dealing with performance suggests that profitability and growth are the important variables. Persistently high profit rates encourage entry while high losses encourage exit and/or discourage new entrants. Growth, especially high rate of growth, tends to encourage entry. Established firms lack excess capacity that serves the dual purpose of accommodating demand increases and viably threatening potential entrants to stay out.

The third factor is economic considerations and includes significant cost differences, capital requirements, economies of scale, and product differentiation. Oligopoly literature contains an extensive discussion as to why and how these factors may serve as barriers to entry.

The fourth factor is informational uncertainties, which originate with the problem that potential entrants not only lack adequate information on current market and production conditions but may not be able to deal with changes in these variables. Not only are they faced with the risk that they will earn less than the competitive return as a result, but also that they will be forced out with significant losses.

The fifth factor deals essentially with the issue that entry is basically a disequilibrium process requiring expenditures of time and resources to move from one competitive stage to another. Lawsuits, cost overrides, and loss of important opportunities are time consuming and expensive. The net effect is to raise barriers to entry.

The sixth factor is the strategic behavior of "established firms threatened with market penetration including the decision to ignore, prevent, delay, accommodate, or fight entry."[10] The choice of a specific option depends on how the practical and economic consequences flowing from that option are evaluated.

NOTES

1. See, for example, Peter F. Drucker, "Multinationals and Developing Countries: Myths and Realities," *Foreign Affairs*, October 1974, pp. 121-34.

2. See, for example, N. Hood and S. Young, *The Economics of the Multi-National Enterprise* (New York: Longman, 1979).

3. Hood and Young, *The Economics of the Multi-National Enterprise*; in addition, see F. Stubenitsky, *American Direct Investment in the Netherlands Industry* (Rotterdam: Rotterdam University Press, 1970); J. N. Behrman, *Some Patterns in the Rise of the Multinational Enterprise* (Chapel Hill: Graduate School of Business Administration, University of North Carolina, 1970); Y. Aharoni, *The Foreign Investment Decision Process* (Cambridge, Mass.: Harvard University Press, 1966); C. P. Kindelberger, ed., *The International Corporation* (Cambridge, Mass.: MIT Press, 1970); J. S. Arpan, "Multinational Firm Pricing in International Markets," *Sloan Management Review*, Winter 1972-73; J. H. Dunning, "Multinational Enterprises, Market Structures, Economic Power and Industrial Power," *Journal of World Trade Law*, November-December 1974.

4. Hood and Young, *The Economics of the Multinational Enterprise*; and J. E. S. Parker, *The Economics of Innovation: The National and International Enterprise in Technological Change* (London: Longman, 1974).

5. United Nations, Department of Economic and Social Affairs, *The Impact of Multinational Corporations on Development and on International Relations*, E/SSOD, Rev. 1 (ST/ESA16) (New York: United Nations, 1974).

6. George W. Ball, "The Relations of the Multinational Corporation to the 'Host' State," in *Global Companies: The Political Economy of World Business*, edited by George W. Ball (Englewood Cliffs, N.J.: Prentice-Hall, American Assembly, 1975), p. 65.

7. *Restrictive Business Practices of Multinational Enterprises*, Report of the Committee of Experts on Restrictive Business Practices (Paris: OECD, 1977).

8. Ibid.

9. Kofi O. Nti and Martin Shubik, "Entry in Oligopoly Theory: A Survey," *Eastern Economic Journal*, January-April 1979, pp. 271-89.

10. Ibid., p. 284.

9

THE MONETARY APPROACH
TO EXTERNAL ECONOMIC RELATIONS:
LIMITS TO NATIONAL SOVEREIGNTY

THE ISSUE

Economic nationalism or mercantilism favors various interventions of various kinds into international trade. In early mercantilism, as we have discussed, these interventions were viewed as a means for accumulating specie (gold and silver) and building up the nation's political and military power. The classical school rejected this view on the basis of two principles that have been incorporated into the main body of economics.

First, David Hume presented his now famous price-specie flow mechanism, according to which, in the long run, a nation has no control over the quantity of the domestic money supply for the simple reason that the public can import or export specie in exchange for imports or exports of domestic goods and services. In the modern counterpart, as this chapter discusses, the principle is the same. The nation can control the ratio of its international reserves to its domestic supply, and therefore the amount of its international reserves, through the control its central bank can exercise over the volumes of domestic credit outstanding against its money. In addition, the public can adjust actual to desired money supply through international transactions in securities as well as in goods and services.

Second is Adam Smith's principle of specialization and division of labor, which, as applied to international trade, implies that free trade rather than the mercantilist policies of government intervention in trade is the welfare-maximizing policy a nation should follow. Our earlier discussion suggests that the exceptions to this principle include the infant industry argument of List and others. Other exceptions include the optimum tariff whereby a country could exploit monopoly or monopsony power and turn its terms of trade in its favor at the expense of restricting its trade. There are also minor exceptions to which classical and neoclassical economists will admit. This chapter, however, focuses Hume's principle and the monetary approach to a country's external constraints to national sovereignty.

THE APPROACH

In economies that are highly dependent upon foreign trade—as are the small nations and emerging countries—international reserve levels are positively related to the level of domestic income and the exchange rate and negatively related to the domestic component of the monetary base.[1] Over the long run, moreover, the money supply grows at a rate that maintains equilibrium in the balance of payments. Furthermore, although the monetary authorities can influence short-term movements in the money supply, they cannot, however, indefinitely counteract long-term excess money stocks unless they are willing from time to time to change the country's foreign exchange rate.

The monetary approach to issues involving the balance of payments in small open economies is particularly suitable. In these countries and emerging countries as well, control over domestic credit is utilized as a major instrument of money management and balance-of-payments control. Typically, it is credit expansion that is the cause of the balance-of-payments problems in these countries. The reasons for such an expansion of credit, of course, can be diverse—for example, public development expenditures, expansion and construction of other productive facilities. Whatever the reasons are, the authorities are not absolved from ultimate responsibility.

Many of these countries have relatively simple monetary and financial structures so that there are fewer alternatives to holding funds in monetary form or spending them on domestic or foreign goods and services or foreign financial obligations.[2] To this may be added that the analytical framework of analysis itself is easier to accommodate to available data in these countries.

By integrating the current and capital accounts of the balance of payments and focusing on the demand and not the supply for money and their consequent influence on reserve positions, the monetary approach argues that a small nation can maintain a negative current account and yet promote balance-of-payments stability through attraction of capital inflows.[3] Through appropriate monetary management, small nations as well as emerging nations can create a stable environment so as to attract external resources that may be used for development, among other purposes. This serves to underscore our discussion on the importance of maintaining a stable monetary environment. Such an environment will serve to attract reserves through the capital account and thus can be utilized to offset current account imports.

If growth is accompanied by a stable monetary policy so as to permit the inflow of foreign reserves into the current account, the foreign exchange gap expressed in some economic development literature can be reduced if not indeed eliminated.[4] In essence, monetary stability is a positive influence on a country's foreign exchange position. This stability, moreover, can be achieved with a minimum of discretionary intervention on the part of monetary authorities, whose imperfect knowledge, especially in emerging countries, leaves much to be desired. We shall have more to say about monetary arrangements elsewhere.

THEORETICAL FRAMEWORK

The monetary theory of the balance of payments interprets surpluses and deficits as results of excess demands and supplies of money in a country.[5] The theory argues that international or interregional money flows eliminate the surpluses or deficits and so create balance-of-payments equilibrium and monetary equilibrium at the same time. It stresses the stability of money demand and supply functions. The theory is, in fact, an extension of the monetarist quantity theory. It encompasses the gold standard or gold exchanges standards of years past as well as contemporary fiat money standards with regimes of floating or flexible exchange rates such as have existed since 1973.

To be sure, the "law of one price" or Purchasing Power Parity Theory (PPP) is an important (if not critical) element in the monetarist approach to the balance of payments. What is important is that after allowing for transportation costs, tariffs, and similar items, prices of identical goods will be equalized in the long run. There may very well be departures in the prices for these goods in the short run. In the long run, however, arbitrage will ensure equality. The analysis is more complicated by the existence of traded and nontraded goods. This does not, however, invalidate the results.

The PPP Theory combines with the monetary approach to the balance of payments to explain movements of international exchange rates between national currencies over both the short and long run. The essential proposition of the theory is that, in the long run, exchange rates adjust to the relative purchasing powers of different national currencies, which in turn are determined by relative demands and supplies of domestic currencies. Exchange rates are, in the final analysis, determined by factors that affect the demand for money, such as interest rates, real income, and the money supply in each country. The PPP Theory thus argues that, as a consequence, monetary authorities have little direct influence on exchange rates.

Inflationary expectations play an important role, especially in the short-run theory. For instance, a well-known proposition in economics is Irving Fisher's argument that nominal interest rates equal the real interest rate and the expected rate of inflation. By the extension of the law of one price to international capital markets, and except for differences in risks and cost of transporting loanable funds between markets, competition for borrowing and lending should equalize the real rate of interest.

Nevertheless, people will not readily lend abroad if they expect a high rate of inflation abroad to erode the purchasing power of the principal sum of their loans. As a result, nominal interest rates will adjust in order to reflect expected rates of inflation in each country. These expectations are reflections of traders in international money and capital markets and their expectations of excessive monetary growth in various countries.[6] The higher the expected excess monetary growth (other things being equal), the higher will be the expected rate of inflation and the higher will be nominal interest rates relative to those elsewhere.

We can express the monetary approach more formally as follows: assume full employment in each country so that national income stays fixed at Y at home and Y* abroad. Domestic and foreign price levels are P and P*, nominal money supplies are M and M*. Assume also that the velocity of money, V and V*, is given and independent of the interest rate. Then the domestic and foreign demands for money are respectively:

$$M = (1/V)PY \text{ and } M* = (1/V*)P*Y* \qquad (1)$$

Rearranging these expressions, the price levels are

$$P = V(M/Y) \text{ and } P* = V*(M*/Y*) \tag{2}$$

If E is the exchange rate that is the price of foreign currency, and absolute PPP holds, then $P = EP*$, or $E = P/P*$. Substituting, we get:

$$E = (\frac{M}{M*}) \ (\frac{V}{V*}) \ (\frac{Y}{Y*}) \tag{3}$$

Domestic currency depreciates (that is, E rises) if the domestic money supply grows faster than that abroad, domestic real income grows more slowly than that abroad, or the domestic velocity coefficient increases relative to that abroad.

The theory may be extended so as to take into account that velocity (reciprocal of the demand for money) depends on real income and the alternative cost of holding money.[7]

$$V = Y^{n-1} \exp(\theta r) \tag{4}$$

where r is the nominal rate of interest. The functional form is a matter of expositional convenience and monetary tradition.

Substituting equation (4) into (3) and taking logs, we obtain the standard equation of the monetary approach:

$$e = m-m* + \lambda(y-y*) + \theta(r-r*) \tag{5}$$

where e, m, and m* are logarithms of the corresponding capital letter variables.

Equation (5) says that an increase in domestic money stock or a decline in domestic relative income will lead to a depreciation, as would a rise in domestic interest rates. The conclusion that a rise in interest rates will lead to depreciation is contrary to received doctrine, which holds that the exchange rate will appreciate. The explanation is as follows: An increase in interest rates reduces the demand for real cash balances. Given the nominal stock of money, the price level must increase to reduce the real stock of money to its lower equilibrium level. Since domestic prices are rising and thus out of line with those of other countries, a depreciation is required to restore PPP.

EMPIRICAL EVIDENCE

How consistent is the monetary approach to the balance of payments with available empirical evidence? To answer this we shall draw briefly on the studies of Putman, Zecher, D. Sykes Wilford, and Walton T. Wilford on international reserve flows and Macesich and Tsai's investigation of the United States, Canada, and Mexico.[8]

The model developed by Putnam and Wilford is also examined by Wilford and Zecher for Mexico. This model is also tested by Macesich and Tsai against the floating exchange rate experience of the United States, Canada, and Mexico. The basic reserve flow equation is:

$$(\frac{R}{H})gR = b_0 + b_1 gY + b_2 gr + b_3 gP + b_4 ga + b_5 (\frac{D}{H}) gD + u \qquad (6)$$

where: $gX = d\ln X/dt$ = the rate of growth in country j of X: $X = R_1$ Y_1 P_1 r, a, D and:

P = price level
r = interest rate
Y = real income
u = a log normal distributed disturbance term
a = the money multiplier
R = the stock of international reserves
D = domestic credit

The annual data for the period 1973-80 are from the IMF's International Financial Statistics. Interest rates are comparable for Canada, Mexico, and the United States, and the price variables are the individual consumer price indexes. The real income variable is nominal GNP deflated by the consumer price index. Money supplies are narrowly defined.

In addition to estimating equations specified solely with domestic prices and interest rates as proxies for the world price level and interest rate, the purchasing power parity and interest rate parity assumptions are integrated directly into the reduced form tests as suggested by Putnam and Wilford. Thus, U.S. price levels and interest rates that also serve as proxies for world variables are substituted for domestic variables. This specification follows from the hypothesis that "the world's financial markets ensure interest arbitrage such that movements in any interest rates (the U.S. rate specifically) reflect the underlying real factors which cause a portfolio holder to demand money."[9] Results for the floating exchange rate regime, 1973-80, are drawn from the Macesich and Tsai study, where U.S. prices and interest rates are used as "proxies" for world variables.

Further, the stock of high-powered money, H_i in country j, is defined in two different ways:

H_i = international reserves (foreign exchanges) + domestic credit

or

H_i = net foreign assets (monetary survey) + domestic credit

For the floating exchange period, results reported by Macesich and Tsai are less satisfactory than reported by Wilford, Putnam, Zecher, and others for the fixed exchange rate period. Most of the F-values are not significant at the 0.05 level. However, when high-powered money is defined as a sum of the net foreign assets and domestic credit, the results for Canada and Mexico are superior. All F-values are highly significant at the 0.05 level. The R^2 s range from .9491 to .9980. Most of the regression coefficients are significantly different from zero for Canada and Mexico. However, the signs of the coefficients for most of the variables are not in conformity with the theory. These results may be due to drastic changes in the Mexican economic structure and its foreign economic policy during the period 1973-80. There is additional evidence in the fact that U.S. prices and interest rates seem to have a rather significant effect on the Mexican and Canadian balance-of-payments equilibrium.

Additional insight into the exchange rate issue may be had by testing a simple static equilibrium model of exchange rate determination proposed by Humphrey and Lawler.[10] The model states that the bilateral exchange rate between any two national currencies is determined by relative money stocks, relative real income, and relative nominal interest rates—the last variable reflecting expectational influences that enter into exchange rate determination. In other words, the interest rate variable reflects relative expectations regarding national inflationary prospects.

The following reduced-form exchange rate equation is estimated and used by Macesich and Tsai to explain the behavior of the United States/Canada, United States/Mexico, and Canada/Mexico exchange rates, respectively, over the post-1972 period of generalized floating:

$$\ln x = a_0 + a_1 \ln(M/M^0) - a_2 \ln(Y/Y^0) + a_3 \ln(r/r^0) \tag{7}$$

where X = the exchange rate (defined as the domestic currency price of a unit foreign currency)

Y = real income
M = nominal money stock (assumed to be exogenously determined by the central bank)
r = nominal rate of interest

O = omicrons used to distinguish foreign country variables from home variables

a_1 = coefficients to be estimated from the statistical data.

It is noted that a priori expected values of the coefficients attached to the money and income variables are unity, whereas the coefficients attached to the interest rate variables should lie between zero and unity. Annual data for the period 1973-80 are used in the analysis.

The empirical results are, in general, consistent with the theoretical model. All of the coefficients on the explanatory variables have the expected signs, except the coefficients on United States/Canada interest rates. All coefficients on Mexico/United States money stock, real income, and interest rate variables are statistically significantly different from zero at the 0.01 level. However, the Canada/Mexico coefficient on real income is not significantly different from zero at the 0.01 level. The results for Canada/United States exchange rate are less satisfactory. Only the coefficients on money stock and real income (when M_1 is used) are significant at the 0.01 level. Thus, the empirical results obtained by Macesich and Tsai seem to support the simple model of exchange rate determination developed by Humphrey and Lawler. These results suggest that the model is a fairly accurate description of floating exchange rate regimes, at least for the Mexico/United States and Canada/Mexico exchange rates.

Walton T. Wilford summarizes in his study a survey of results for a number of small Third World countries.[11] These results are particularly useful for the purposes at hand. They appear consistent with the hypothesis advanced by the monetary approach to the balance of payments that "international reserve levels are positively related to the level of domestic income and exchange rate, and negatively related to the domestic component of the monetary base."[12] The summary results imply, moreover, that in economies "highly dependent upon foreign trade, as are the developing countries, the money supply grows at a rate that over the long run, maintains an equilibrium in the foreign balance."[13] And finally, the monetary authorities cannot over the long-run influence excess money stocks unless they are also willing to change the exchange rate.

To be sure, many of the country studies reported on by Wilford cover the fixed exchange rate period prior to 1973. Since 1973, however, many countries have moved to more flexible rates. Nevertheless for small nations as well as emerging nations it is useful as a first approximation to consider these nations as though they are de facto on a regime of fixed exchange rates. Many have their currencies closely tied to the currencies of larger countries—for example, the Austrian schilling and the West German mark. For the most part, these countries are price takers in world goods, services, and capital. Thus they are constrained in their operations in the international economic arena.

Insight into the extent and nature of this constraint is suggested by a National Bureau of Economic Research study by Darby et al. of how inflation was transmitted among countries during the Bretton Woods fixed exchange rate period.[14] For the most part, the study covers the period 1955-76 and includes the United States, the United Kingdom, Canada, France, Germany, Italy, Japan, and the Netherlands. According to the study, monetary factors are responsible for the worldwide inflation during this period. Such special factors as OPEC-induced oil price rises in 1973-74, the monopoly power of business and unions, and the substantial rise in commodity prices account for only a small part of the inflation.

The inflation of the 1960s and 1970s was a monetary phenomenon, and a key role was played by the United States. Its excessive monetary growth was exported abroad via the fixed exchange rate system in existence de facto until 1973. This is, in fact, consistent with monetarist ideas discussed earlier.

The oil-shock hypothesis advanced by some people receives limited empirical support in this study. Increased oil prices can affect the general price level, either by decreasing the real quantity of money demanded or by increasing the nominal quantity of money supplied. Indeed, the oil shock appears to account at most for 1 percent of the 3.5 percent increase in the average 1971-75 inflation rate over 1966-70.

If acceleration of money growth is the major cause of worldwide inflation, the evidence points to the United States, the reserve country, as the culprit. In the first instance, international factors accounted for little in the Federal Reserve's money supply reaction function. Indeed, variations in the U.S. money growth were a cause of its balance-of-payments flows, which affected domestic money growth in the seven other countries but not in the United States.

Moreover, growth in real money demanded in the United States is stable over long periods, even though it is responsive to money and other shocks in the short run. According to the reported results for four-year averages, variations in nominal money growth explain some 97 percent of the variations in postwar U.S. inflation. In effect, the acceleration of the trend rate of U.S. inflation is domestic and not international in origin.

Evidence is also provided by Darby et al. as to whether induced reserve flows were completely or partially sterilized during the Bretton Woods era. Monetarists argue that sterilization is impossible in the long run. The level of foreign currency reserves provides a limit to the duration of time a deficit country can finance a deficit and therefore sterilize the monetary effects. However, it is not clear that there are similar pressures on a surplus country that is continually acquiring reserves. To be sure, it is irrational for a country to pursue a long-run policy of achieving continuous balance-of-payments surplus, for it means that it is willing to trade goods and services for foreign balances without limit.

According to Darby et al.'s evidence, which is based upon three separate investigations of sterilization, partial or complete sterilization appears to have been a general practice for the set of industrialized nonreserve countries studied. Their finding is consistent with short-run sterilization and a pattern of lagged adjustments. They consider as well an important conclusion of the monetary approach to the balance of payments: Nonreserve central banks are unimportant with respect to their domestic money supplies and interest rates, but can attain any desired balance of payments via their actions. This conclusion is based on the following assumptions: Goods are perfect substitutes internationally, and assets are perfect substitutes. Darby et al. add a third assumption—that expectations of depreciation are also responsive to variations in the balance of payments. Any one of these three conditions, along with others, precludes effective monetary control. As such, it is difficult to test conclusively the importance of nonreserve bank control with respect to their money supplies.

Nevertheless, the authors conclude that nonreserve central banks did in fact exercise monetary control under pegged exchange rates. They argue that the direct evidence on the two major conditions indicated that neither goods nor assets were perfect substitutes internationally. According to their interpretation, the evidence was incontrovertible that the actual growth in the money supply was determined, in part, by domestic policy goals.

As a result, Darby et al. conclude that the adjustment process under the Bretton Woods system can be characterized roughly as follows: First, international factors as such played a minor role in the U.S. monetary and inflationary trends. These were determined largely by domestic factors. Second, the proximate determination of inflation in the nonreserve countries was found to be in their own past money supply growth. Third, changes in money growth in the United States did not lead to significant capital outflows. Trade-flow effects built up as a result of inflation shifted price levels. Fourth, these balance-of-payments flows did not significantly impact on the nonreserve country money growth. Their cumulative lagged effected could be very important.

In fact, they argue, it is this long cumulative lag from U.S. money growth to an increase in inflation in nonreserve countries that can explain the failure of the Bretton Woods system. According to the study, the increase in U.S. inflation at the onset of the 1966-70 period had little impact on inflation rates in the nonreserve countries. As the U.S. inflation continued, however, relative price levels shifted by some 8 percent. The nonreserve countries responded with a lag, and their money growth rates began to rise in response to growing balance-of-payments surpluses.

The inflation rates of these countries responded only with an additional lag. Eventually the large surpluses of the late 1960s and early 1970s generated a money growth that was sufficient to outpace U.S. inflation in 1971-75. The inflation so generated offset about half of the 8 percent change in relative price levels that had occurred in 1966-70. These surpluses, however, became so large as to produce speculative capital flows and a breakdown of the Bretton Woods system.

To make matters worse, the inflation rate targets of the Federal Reserve system and nonreserve banks were not in harmony. Had they been so, the lagged adjustment process outlined above might have been equal to the relatively small stress implied by once-and-for-all shifts in purchasing power. As Darby et al. point out, however, the strong upward trend in the U.S. money supply reaction function was closer to such countries as Great Britain and Italy, which preferred faster money supply growth. Furthermore, the United States at the same time parted from such countries as Germany, which preferred a lower money supply growth and a lower rate of inflation.

The essential message Darby et al. underscore is that controlling inflation reduces to the problem of controlling the money supply. This is technically possible, although central banks were not directed to do so by any constitutional requirement establishing a specific money growth rule or fixing the exchange rate between money and either a commodity or the currency of a country fixed in terms of such a commodity.

The special position of the United States as a reserve currency country also suggests the asymmetry of the Bretton Woods system. The feedback from the reserve currency country (in this case the United States) and its balance of payments to its money supply is broken. Other countries were willing to acquire certain liquid assets drawn on the United States and to regard these as reserve assets. An expansionary monetary policy by the reserve country may have no effect on its balance of payments; its trading partners will register a surplus in their balance of payments, leading to an inflow of foreign exchange reserves. One result is that the money supply becomes controllable by the monetary authorities in the currency reserve country. In effect, monetary policy has a domestic impact for a reserve country under fixed and flexible exchange rates, in both the short and long run. Monetary policies in nonreserve countries have limited value since they are compelled, at least in the long run, to accept the rate of monetary expansion originating in the reserve country if they wish to remain on fixed exchange rates.

Since 1973 the world has passed over to a system of managed floating, which is somewhere between a fixed and a flexible exchange rate system. As a result, monetary policy affects both a country's balance of payments and its exchange rate. The important issue is the degree of government intervention. If government intervention is limited to "extreme circumstances" (which is, in fact, what the Reagan administration has adopted), the situation is similar to a flexible exchange rate system. On the other hand, if government intervention to manage the exchange rate is more than an occasional venture, then the situation is fairly close to a fixed exchange rate regime.

NOTES

1. See Harry G. Johnson, *Further Essays in Monetary Economics* (Cambridge, Mass.: Harvard University Press, 1973); Robert A. Mundell, *International Economics* (New York: Macmillan, 1968); B. H. Putnam and D. Sykes Wilford, eds., *The Monetary Approach to International Adjustment* (New York: Praeger, 1978); Jacob A. Frenkel and Harry G. Johnson, eds., *The Monetary Approach to the Balance of Payments* (London: George Allen and Unwin, 1976); George Macesich, *Monetarism: Theory and Policy* (New York: Praeger, 1983).

2. D. Dimitrijević and George Macesich, *Money and Finance in Yugoslavia: A Comparative Analysis* (New York: Praeger, 1983).

3. See Walton T. Wilford, "Some Observations on the Monetary Approach to Balance of Payments and the Third World," in Putnam and Wilford, *The Monetary Approach to International Adjustment*, pp. 98-116.

4. Ibid.

5. Macesich, *Monetarism*, Chapter 10.

6. See Jacob A. Frenkel, "A Monetary Approach to the Exchange Rate: Doctrinal Aspects and Empirical Evidence," in *The Economics of Exchange Rates*, edited by Jacob A. Frenkel and Harry G. Johnson (Reading, Mass.: Addison-Wesley, 1978), pp. 1-25; John F. O. Bilson, "The Current Experience with Floating Exchange Rates: An Appraisal of the Monetary Approach," *American Economic Review*, May 1978, pp. 392-97; Frenkel, "The Forward Exchange Rate, Expectations and the Demand for Money: The German Hyperinflation," *American Economic Review*, September 1977, pp. 653-70; Frenkel, "Purchasing Power Parity: Doctrinal Perspective and Evidence from the 1920's," *Journal of International Economics*, May 1978, pp. 169-91; Frenkel, "Exchange Rates, Prices and Money: Lessons from the 1920's," *American Economic Review*, May 1980, pp. 235-42; John F. O. Bilson, "Profitability and Stability in International Currency Markets," Working Paper No. 664, April 1981, National Bureau of Economic Research. In addition to the Bilson paper cited above, see also Peter B. Kenan, "New Views of Exchange Rates and Old Views of Policy," Norman C. Miller, "Monetary vs. Traditional Approaches of Balance of Payments Analysis," and the discussion by Rudiger Dornbusch, Jacob A. Frenkel, and Marc C. Miles in *American Economic Review*, May 1978, pp. 398-416.

7. For this account, see Rudiger Dornbusch, "Monetary Policy under Exchange-Rate Flexibility," in *Managed Exchange Rate Flexibility: The Recent Experience*, edited by J. R. Artus et al. (Boston: Federal Reserve Bank of Boston, 1978), pp. 90-122.

8. Bluford H. Putnam and D. Sykes Wilford, "International Reserve Flows: Seemingly Unrelated Regressions," and Walton T. Wilford, "Some Observations on the Monetary Approach to Balance of Payments and Third World Countries," in Putnam and Wilford, *The Monetary Approach to International Adjustment*, pp. 71-84; George Macesich and H. Tsai, "A North American Common Market: The Issue of Independent Monetary Policy," a paper presented at the North American Economic Society Association meeting in Washington, D.C., December 27-29, 1981; D. Sykes Wilford and J. Richard Zecher, "Monetary Policy and Balance of Payments in Mexico, 1955-75," *Journal of Money, Credit and Banking*, August 1979, pp. 340-48. The reader is referred to the Putnam, Wilford, and Zecher studies and, specifically, for the fixed exchange rate period before 1973, for a detailed discussion of the issues.

9. Putnam and Wilford, "International Reserve Flows."

10. Thomas M. Humphrey and Thomas A. Lawler, "Factors Determining Exchange Rates: A Simple Model and Empirical Tests," in Putnam and Wilford, *The Monetary Approach to International Adjustment*, pp. 134-45.

11. W. T. Wilford, "Some Observations."

12. Ibid., p. 113.

13. Ibid.

14. Michael Darby, James R. Lothian, Arthur Gandalfi, Anna J. Schwartz, and Alan C. Stockman, *The International Transmission of Inflation* (forthcoming,

National Bureau of Economic Research). See also Bluford H. Putnam and D. Sykes Wilford, "Money, Income and Causality in the United States and the United Kingdom: A Theoretical Explanation of Different Findings," *American Economic Review*, June 1978, pp. 423-27; Terry C. Mills and Geoffrey E. Wood, "Money-Income Relationships and the Exchange Rate Regime," *Review*, Federal Reserve Bank of St. Louis, August 1978, pp. 22-27; Thomas D. Willet, *International Liquidity Issues* (Washington, D.C.: American Enterprise Institute for Public Policy Research, 1980); Lance Girton and Don Roper, "A Monetary Model and Exchange Market Pressure Applied to the Post-war Canadian Experience," *American Economic Review*, September 1977, pp. 537-48; Stephen P. Magee, "The Empirical Evidence on the Monetary Approach to the Balance of Payments and Exchange Rates," *American Economic Review*, May 1976, pp. 163-70.

10

PROVIDING FOR A
STABLE MONETARY FRAMEWORK

ECONOMIC NATIONALISM AND THE
INTERNATIONAL ENVIRONMENT

Economic nationalism received an impetus with the collapse of the international monetary system in the 1930s. The importance of maintaining a stable monetary system is underscored by events that led to its collapse. The subsequent tendency on the part of major trading countries to allow their currencies to become overvalued encouraged interventionist and parochial nationalist economic policies to improve the balance of payments and/or remedy the unemployment resulting from deflationary policies aimed at preserving the exchange rate. Cases in point are Great Britain in the prewar period and the United States. Germany and Japan are additional postwar examples of major trading countries engaging in de facto mercantilist policies of using currency undervaluation to generate domestic employment by means of a balance-of-payments surplus.

These nationalist policies continue to remain important in the trading world even as more sophisticated versions of these policies are manifest in the relatively new concern over economic growth and development based on advanced technology.[1] These more sophisticated versions of mercantilist policies and economic nationalism owe much to the increasing role of government and bureaucracy in the national economy. Not only do these policies discriminate against foreign industries but also they discriminate between categories of domestic industries according to their presumed growth potential. Elements of

143

the older infant industry argument for protection against imports are integrated with the need to cultivate high technology industries for export as a means for increasing comparative advantage. Unfortunately for this view, the empirical evidence does not support it. There is no simple theory of how to promote economic growth or to justify a simple policy recommendation.

Thus the crude protective tariff of traditional mercantilism as a means of protecting domestic industry does indeed give way to more sophisticated means. Given the economic powers at the disposal of the contemporary nation-state, there is now a shortage of means to do so. Indeed, in the case of industries based on high technology with important economies of scale and diminishing costs as overhead R & D investment is spread over a larger volume of output, protection of domestic output in the domestic national market is no longer feasible. In order to be adequate and efficient it is necessary to extend protection to the export market. The methods for doing so include subsidization of export credit rather than exports themselves; subsidization of research and development costs for promising export industries; tying various foreign assistance programs to purchases from domestic suppliers; escalated tariffs; restriction on migration to prevent "brain drain." These are only the more obvious methods available to the nation-state in pursuit of mercantilist policies and economic nationalism.

Postwar efforts toward world free trade through multilateral tariff-reducing negotiations under the General Agreement on Tariffs and Trade (GATT) have not been freely realized. To many observers GATT inspires little confidence and less respect. It is overly legalistic. Its rules do not adequately address key trade problems such as agriculture, investment-related distortions, and government support for key sectors. It is frequently bypassed or ignored as countries unilaterally, bilaterally, or in small groups take actions that violate its spirit and substance.

As a result, free trade is viewed as more of a myth than a reality. A nation-state cannot easily claim that GATT rules prohibit it from taking steps to protect or subsidize domestic interests when its citizens see violations of those rules by other nations. This is not the fault of GATT itself; it simply reflects the policies and objectives of member nation-states.

Member nations, unfortunately, have sought to stretch, avoid, or unilaterally interpret GATT rules so as to maintain latitude enough to impose subsidies or other protective measures in response to domestic constituencies. As a result they have weakened the world trading system's ability, and their own, to encourage restraint and its capacity to restore fair and open trade. They have thus restored and promoted mercantilist policies. In doing so they have done considerable harm to their own long-term interests.

It is imperative, particularly for small nation-states and emerging countries, that GATT—which is based on admirable principles—be made to work better. There should be absolutely no trade discrimination. Every country should get the same terms extended to the "most favored nation." The use of quantitative restrictions should be condemned. Any disagreements should be resolved through consultation, not trade warfare.

It is, moreover, important that these principles of free trade be clarified so as to avoid the many ambiguities subject to various interpretations that exist in GATT. It may well be that simple arrangements could be incorporated into GATT to limit trade distortions while avoiding the complex legalities and delays that characterize the current system.

A number of proposals for improving GATT are available. One suggests that before imposing new trade restrictions or trade subsidies, or taking other actions that would materially affect trade, nations would be required to notify a GATT or GATT-affiliated consultative monitoring committee that would be continuously in session.[2] The country would be required to justify the proposed measure, work out with other affected countries ways of avoiding or offsetting any injury to them, indicate the planned duration of the measure, provide a schedule for phasing it down and out, and submit a credible program to improve competitiveness of the relevant domestic industry while the measure is in place. This is certainly a good step in the direction of free trade.

Attention is called to barriers to trade caused by GATT's encouragement in the formation of regional trade organizations. A case in point is the European Economic Community, which Harry Johnson describes as "the epitome of modernized mercantilism."[3] The issue at hand is GATT's exception to the general principle of nondiscrimination for customs unions and free trade areas, presumably because 100 percent discriminatory trading arrangements among groups of nations against outsiders can be automatically construed as a step toward freer world trade. Whether this is indeed such a step rests on the issue between increasing total international trade by reducing protection of domestic producers and diverting trade away from nonmembers toward partners in the arrangement.

Indeed, Common Market membership appealed to the self-interest of British industry, seeing in it a community home market protected against U.S. competition.[4] Even though the interests of the British public would have been better served by free trade or by association with the United States, the issue, according to Common Market supporters, is political and not economic. Johnson succinctly summarizes Britain's entrance into the Common Market:

> Unable to broach the fundamental political question—of Europe versus America—the Labour Party was forced into futile quibbling about the tactics of obtaining common market entry without being able to question the strategy, and the decision went by default as a carefully stage-managed non-debate over non-issues.[5]

None of this has gone unnoticed in the emerging nations of the Third World. As we have discussed, they too have mounted policies of economic nationalism as a defense against foreign penetration and/or to secure trade advantages. Unfortunately such policies promise to reduce significantly their opportunities to promote their economic development through competition in a large, liberal, and impersonal international market. They are, as indeed are all trading countries, well advised to examine carefully the use of such measures as taxing and subsidizing and general regulatory powers as methods for promoting economic nationalism.

These methods are indeed more efficient protective substitutes for the crude tariff and quota instruments of the past, as is the pursuit of protectionist aims through the formation of supranational trading blocs. They represent, nonetheless, misguided policies whose antecedents are firmly lodged in mercantilist doctrine and economic nationalism.

Many of the emerging nations base their hopes on the United Nations Conference on Trade and Development, but the developed industrial nations are not all sympathetic to UNCTAD. In their view, the organization is unrealistic and unbalanced in its criticism of industrial countries and too prone to accept statist approaches to economic problems—for example, compulsory transfer of technology.

For their part the emerging nations often feel mistreated and ignored by the richer nations. They believe the North-South dialogue has been wrongly interpreted by the North. Many, in fact, feel that political and social troubles in the emerging nations will free the industrial nations to renew the dialogue. Famine in Africa and difficulties in developing-debtor countries are but cases in point.

They deny that UNCTAD is dominated by "socialist thinking." They argue that since many of the emerging nations have a "mixed economy" with both private and public sectors, government gets into economic areas more readily than in developed countries, apart even from the need to build infrastructures such as roads, airports, and highways.

The United States and other industrial countries insist that the dialogue take place within the IMF-World Bank framework, where their weighted voting power has control, rather than in UNCTAD, where one nation-one vote gives the developing countries a hugh majority.

With Third World debt totaling close to $800 billion, resolution of individual country debt problems is essential to an ultimate solution of the world debt imbroglio. UNCTAD would like to see a reduction in protectionism by the industrial countries. It would also like to see the industrial nations send more resources to the poorer nations by strengthening the World Bank, the IMF, and other such multilateral institutions. It also calls for lower interest rates on developing country debts and stretching repayments over a longer period, as has been done with Mexico. Its members would also like to see other debt-easing steps, such as a cap on interest rates and a facility within IMF to compensate poor countries for higher interest rates. In their view UNCTAD provides a useful forum in which developing countries, industrial nations, and socialist nations can discuss and negotiate common economic problems.

There is thus a need, indeed an urgency, to view the problems of the world economy within an international context. This was done in the closing years of World War II in the Bretton Woods Conference. This conference stands as an attempt to cope with world monetary, trade, investment, and debt problems in an international fashion. The rehabilitation of this concept would provide a constructive alternative to contemporary creeping mercantilism and economic nationalism. This is one alternative; there are others.

For instance, I argue elsewhere in connection with the ongoing dialogue between developing-debtor countries and developed-creditor countries that world cooperation can indeed work with an appropriate strategy.[6] The strategy, which is provided in the basic framework of the theory of cooperation, is a simple Tit for Tat strategy with the first move being cooperation.

World banks can and do serve as instruments (or clusters) for promoting a Tit for Tat strategy of cooperation. The large debt owed by developing countries to their developed-nation creditors (including banks) can serve to enhance cooperation among nations. It can promote the evaluation of an international environment in which a strategy of cooperation will displace egoistic strategies. World debt is now of a size that assures cooperators the necessary cluster for a strategy of cooperation to be firmly established. Once established it well tend to flourish. It is indeed an opportunity for the world to move up the ratchet of cooperation as the theory of cooperation suggests.

Essential to an evolving environment of cooperation and reciprocity, however, is domestic and international monetary stability. Monetary authorities and central bankers must ensure that the monetary system itself is not a source of world instability.

THE ISSUE OF MONETARY STABILITY: CONFLICTING VIEWS

Thanks to their intellectual antecedents discussed elsewhere in this study, proposals for monetary stability continue to be mired in controversy. Three views dominate the discussions: the Austrian or continental, the Monetarist or classical or neoclassical, and the Keynesian. These controversies have important implications for monetary stability; we will consider, briefly, each one.

Classical and neoclassical economists promoted rules of the gold standard as a means for constraining the international and domestic monetary systems within bounds in order to minimize the chances that money would become a political issue and a source of instability. Even so, they were not always successful. The system's periodic breakdown provides ample testimony on this score.

The nineteenth-century view of society's responsibility to maintain trust and faith in money was supported by the bitter eighteenth-century experiences with monetary manipulation and currency excess. Most classical economists and certainly the "Austrians" underscored society's monetary responsibilities for preserving trust and faith in money. The spirit of the tradition is against the use of discretionary monetary policy for the purpose of exploiting the presumed, short-run nonneutrality of money in order to increase permanently employment and output by increasing the stock of money. Though an arbitrary increase in money, in their view, will not necessarily disrupt relative price permanently, such manipulation sets forces into motion whose consequences for social stability are very serious indeed. Since no human power can guarantee against possible misuse of money-issuing authority, to give such unconstrained authority to government is to invite destruction of the social order. To avoid such temptation it is best to tie paper money to a metal value established by law or the economy.[7]

The use of discretionary policy to exploit the short-run nonneutrality of money is a good illustration of a counterproductive strategy incompatible with our theory of cooperation. Indeed, its tertiary effect is to compromise the monetary authority's credibility, thereby destroying the very environment upon which its success depends. In the process the monetary system itself is cast in doubt.

This does not mean that government intervention per se into the economy and specifically into monetary affairs is somehow peculiar to the twentieth century. On the contrary, as we noted, many classical continental and neoclassical economists devoted considerable effort to the definition of international and domestic monetary systems under which total demand would behave "appropriately." They recognized the optional and political determination of the country's monetary system and the need to constrain it with policy based on rules.

It was Keynes who made the revolt against the predominant view of money respectable. It was George Simmel in Germany and others long before Keynes who first suggested the sources of the revolt and foresaw its likely consequences. They did not see the institution of money in mechanical terms but as a conflict between abstract concepts of money and the social trust on which it rests. Their concern was to elucidate the moral basis of monetary order in contrast to the subversion of morals through money, in the abstract, which was feared. Many were pessimistic that the traditional monetary order would survive the revolt against it. On this score they were not to be disappointed.

Keynes, too, was concerned with monetary stability and the fragile nature of a money-using market economy and the social order that went with it.[8] He was also well aware of the need for trust in the stability of purchasing power if the market mechanism was to function properly. Indeed, to Keynes money is not just another commodity. A money economy is very different from a barter economy. This idea was lost, wrote Laidler and Rowe,

> as the Hicksian IS-LM interpretation of the *General Theory* came to dominate monetary economics, "monetarist" as well as so-called "Keynesian." The dominance of this incomplete version of Keynes in subsequent debates has also surely been the main reason for participants in them having neglected "Austrian" ideas on these matters.[9]

The story, however, is very different on the conduct of monetary policy where Keynes and his followers depart significantly from the Austrian and Monetarist paths. These differences are so profound as to overwhelm areas of agreement. As we have had occasion to note elsewhere, Keynes believed firmly in discretionary monetary policy and viewed the gold standard as a relic. Modern Austrian and some supply-siders hold to the gold standard. Monetarists argue for a given growth rate in the stock of money. The difference between Austrians and Monetarists is essentially about means to achieve agreed-upon ends. The Austrians, while distrusting bureaucrats, are more skeptical than the Monetarists about the stability of the demand for money function and so opt for pegging the price of money in terms of gold, relying on the stability of the relative price of gold in terms of goods in general.

The essence of monetarism then is that money matters a great deal, that it is a key determinant of short-term economic trends. If the money supply behaves erratically, so does the economy. Most economists can accept monetarism in those simple terms. The differences arise, as we noted, when we turn to policy prescription.

To the nonmonetarist the fact that money matters means that it is something to be carefully manipulated by the central bank through discretionary intervention. In the short run, faster money growth is likely to produce lower interest rates. If the objective is lower interest rates, simply speed up the money supply. This also means that banks are using increased reserves to make loans to people. If the objective is increased economic activity, speed up money growth.

It is agreed that typically fast money growth within a year or two can mean higher prices, so it is important to know when to slow money growth. The trouble with this approach, according to the Monetarists, is that we really do not know when to slow money's growth. For one thing, the lags between changes in the money supply growth and the economy are varied and unpredictable. For another, an attempt to fine-tune monetary policy is likely to cause more problems than it solves.

Given such an environment the best the government can do, continue the Monetarists, is to promote steady growth of the money supply at a moderate rate. This rate is roughly equal to the economy's capacity to grow. For the money supply, the Federal Reserve Bank as well as other central banks use M1 (currency plus checking deposits).[10] Concern over "what is money" arguments has also prompted the use of monetary base (currency plus bank reserves) or merely bank reserves as central bank money supply targets. A policy of stable monetary growth would remove money from the political arena and as a source of economic instability.

To be sure, neither the Federal Reserve (the Fed) nor other central banks are "Monetarist" in the sense that Friedman and other Monetarists would like. The differences, however, have narrowed somewhat. They now turn mostly but not completely on the execution of policy. For example, the slowdown in monetary growth carried out by many of the central banks has been erratic and uneven. In the case of the Fed, making a few technical adjustments would presumably get it on the right track.

Some nonmonetarists and antimonetarists, on the other hand, are saying that we should leave money and monetary policy up to the wisdom of the Federal Reserve system. The Fed would go back to trying to police interest rates, although the Fed seems to recognize now that its power to control rates is very limited. The Fed would keep an eye on everything and do the very best it could.

That surely adds up to much more discretionary administrative intervention by the Fed, if only because the central bank would have so many accidental errors to try to correct. This does not fit well with what the Reagan administration has been trying to do—namely, lessen the government's role in the lives of its citizens. It is certainly inconsistent with the view of Monetarists and others seeking lawful policy systems and limitations on the undefined exercise of power by government.

It is, however, appealing to central bankers and consistent with the modern Keynesian approach and discretionary economic intervention without defined guides or policy systems as we have discussed. Money is thus pushed into the political arena to be fought over according to one's ideological and philosophical inclinations. The idea promoted by Keynesians and others is that money and monetary institutions are simply creations of the state and thus are available for manipulation by a government consisting, for the most part, of wise and well-educated people disinterestedly promoting the best interests of society. In essence, it is at best an elitist view of government or at worst a totalitarian government.

It is also characteristic of the type of discretionary interventionism that has grown rapidly since the Keynesian revolution, although it began long before Keynes, as I have discussed elsewhere.[11] The fact is, for several decades now we have been witnessing a conflict between two incompatible concepts of money: money as a tool of the state and money as a symbol of social trust.[12]

The traditional view of money focused on a monetary order that implied a nondiscretionary policy-ordered system whose operation would not be arbitrarily altered by discretionary intervention in favor of particular individuals, groups, or interests. The survival of such a monetary order has long been questioned by some for the reason that it might not prove possible to make it work in terms of specific goals that society should, in their opinion, pursue. This view, shared by Keynes, leads to utopian attempts to make the uncertain certain by control of society according to plan as well as by transformation of man.

To use the monetary system to pursue changing goals and objectives is incompatible with a stable monetary order. It will make it "capricious and uncertain and prey to conflicting and varying political objectives."[13] A monetary policy, writes Frankel, "which is directed to shifting goals—as for example, full employment, economic growth, economic equality or the attempt to satisfy conflicting demands of capital and labour—cannot but vary with the goals adopted."[14] Friedman sums up the issue well: "We are in danger of assigning to monetary policy a larger role than it can perform in danger of asking it to accomplish tasks that it cannot achieve and, as a result, in danger of preventing it from making the contribution that it is capable of making."[15] Intended to reduce uncertainty, monetary manipulation thus actually increases it by casting doubt on the monetary system itself. This is well illustrated in a number of U.S. historical and contemporary episodes.

MONETARY STABILITY AND EMERGING NATIONS

It may be that nationalism in emerging nations serves as an integrative force and the chief propellant of collective efforts to accelerate economic development. Policies promoting economic nationalism, however, may well impose serious costs on the country. These policies have a preference for government intervention and regulation of economic activity. Insofar as they encourage and foster economic inefficiency they reduce the national income of the country. To be sure, nationalism does provide nonpecuniary returns or psychic income to those with a taste for it, though pecuniary returns are foregone as a result of exercising such tastes.

The problem is one of determining the optimum amount of the collective good of nationalism to supply. Some consumers who stand to benefit will want more; others not so favored will want less. Few will agree that the optimal quantity is truly optimal. Even in countries where a free political framework exists, what a consumer-voter chooses in a political market may be significantly different from what he ultimately receives. The correlation between a voter's choice and the expected outcome may be very weak. Efficient political decisions simply require much more information than efficient market decisions. Political decisions tend to affect everyone in the community, unlike decisions in a private market, which affect primarily the consumer and supplier of a given product or service.

Conflicting views on the optimum amount of nationalism desirable, together with disappointment with the economy's performance, increasingly push the government into the formation of prices and wages to assure desired outcomes. This will typically lead to price and wage controls. Since wage and price controls inevitably fail, the system is increasingly driven into collective participatory planning, where wages and prices are determined. This may, in fact, be desired by people arguing in favor of a "mixed economy" and a large or even total government presence in the economy. Such an arrangement, however, offers little chance that the market system will be allowed to play its effective and efficient role. It also lends credence to charges by the developed countries of the "statist" and interventionist bias in many emerging countries, thereby reducing prospects for successful North-South dialogue.

Failure to allow the market system to play its role, as we have discussed, almost assures that money and the monetary system will not be allowed to play a nondiscriminatory and autonomous role within the constraints of a rules-based policy system so necessary to assure the preservation of economic and monetary stability in the country. It assures that money will slip into the political arena and become a political issue. Its manipulation to pursue changing goals and objectives will make money capricious and subject to varying political objectives and incompatible with a stable monetary order. Monetary manipulation thus assures instability and inflation so characteristic of emerging nations.

We have noted the limits to money and monetary policy in emerging countries in our discussion of external constraints to national sovereignty. In effect, the evidence suggests that the money supply in these countries grows at a rate that over the long run maintains an equilibrium in the foreign balance. Monetary authorities cannot over the long run influence excess money stock unless they are also willing to change the exchange rate.

This is consistent with the monetarist or quantity theory position discussed earlier on the importance of so structuring the monetary system that it will not fall prey to manipulation for political purposes. It underscores that money and the monetary system must be allowed to play a nondiscriminatory and autonomous role within the constraints of a rules-based policy system so necessary to assure the preservation of economic and monetary stability in the country. At the same time such a policy system of rules will serve to constrain the bureaucracy, the elite, and other interests from the use of monetary manipulation to serve their immediate interests.

The monetary and financial systems of most emerging nations can indeed benefit from a rules-based policy system. Dimitrijević and Macesich report that changes in the money supply in emerging nations with very different economic systems nevertheless have rapid effects on economic activity, particularly on the general level of prices.[16] In Yugoslavia from 1964 to 1971, for instance, changes in the money supply explained 53 percent of changes in investment expenditures, 18 percent of changes in personal consumption, and 43 percent of changes in total demand for goods and services with only a one-month time lag.[17] Since the mid 1970s the general lead of prices in the country have risen an average 25 percent per year.

The money-printing and -manipulating monopoly of the nation-state is indeed the heart of the bureaucratic system. Given the records of many emerging Third World countries (and others as well), a printing press can be very dangerous. They can either use some stable currency that cannot be printed locally, or return to the gold standard, or constrain their bureaucracies within a lawful rules-based system as discussed and recommended in this study.

NOTES

1. Harry G. Johnson, *On Economics and Society* (Chicago: University of Chicago Press, 1975, paperback ed., 1982), p. 274.

2. R. O. Hormats, "Trade Adjustment That All Could Support," *Wall Street Journal*, September 19, 1984, p. 32.

3. Johnson, *On Economics and Society*, p. 277. See also George Macesich, *Geld politik in einem gemeinsamen europaischen Markt* (Money in the European Common Market) (Baden-Baden: Nomos Velagsgesellschaft, 1972).

4. Johnson, *On Economics and Society*, p. 277.

5. Ibid., p. 278.

6. George Macesich, *World Banking and Finance: Cooperation versus Conflict* (New York: Praeger, 1984).

7. This was a view widely shared. For instance, George Simmel, a German sociologist, in an important but often overlooked study, *The Philosophy of Money*, first published in 1907 in Berlin (*Philsosphie des Geldes*) wrote:

> The most serious repercussions upon exchange transactions will follow from this situation, particularly at the moment when the government's own resources are paid in devalued money. The numerator of the money fraction—the price of commodities—rises proportionally to the increased supply of money only after large quantities of new money have already been spent by the government, which then finds itself confronted again with a redeemed supply of money. The temptation then to make a new issue of money is generally irresistible and the process begins all over again. I mention this only as an example of the numerous and frequently discussed failures of arbitrary issues of paper money, which present themselves as a temptation whenever money is not closely linked with a substance of limited supply. Today we know that only precious metals, and indeed only gold, guarantee the requisite qualities, and in particular the limitation of quantity; and that paper money can escape the dangers of misuse by arbitrary inflation, only if it is tied to metal value established by law or by the economy.

George Simmel, *The Philosophy of Money*, translated by T. Bottomore and D. Frisby with an Introduction by D. Frisby (London and Boston: Routledge and Kegan Paul, 1977), p. 160. See also David Laidler and Nicholas Rowe, "George Simmel's *Philosophy of Money*: A Review Article for Economists," *Journal of Economic Literature*, March 1980, pp. 97-105.

8. See Laidler and Rowe, "George Simmel's *Philosophy of Money*," p. 103.

9. Ibid.

10. For a detailed analysis of definitions of the money supply, see Milton Friedman and Anna J. Schwartz, *Monetary Statistics of the United States* (New York: Columbia University Press for the National Bureau of Economic Research, 1970).

11. George Macesich, *The Politics of Monetarism: Its Historical and Institutional Development* (Totowa, N.J.: Rowman and Allanheld, 1984).

12. See S. Herbert Frankel, *Two Philosophies of Money: The Conflict of Trust and Authority* (New York: St. Martin's Press, 1977), p. 86; and George Macesich, *The International Monetary Economy and The Third World* (New York: Praeger, 1981), Chapter 1.

13. Frankel, *Two Philosophies*, p. 89.

14. Ibid., p. 92.

15. Milton Friedman, "The Role of Monetary Policy," in *The Optimum Quantity of Money and Other Essays*, edited by Milton Friedman (Chicago: Aldine, 1969), p. 99.

16. See D. Dimitrijević and George Macesich, *Money and Finance in Yugoslavia: A Comparative Analysis* (New York: Praeger, 1983).

17. Ibid., p. 108.

INDEX

ABOUT THE AUTHOR

GEORGE MACESICH is Professor of Economics and Director of the Center for Yugoslav-American Studies, Research and Exchanges at the Florida State University in Tallahassee. He received his Ph.D. in economics from the University of Chicago. His books, among others, include *The International Monetary Economy and the Third World* (Praeger), *Monetarism: Theory and Policy, The Politics of Monetarism: Its Historical and Institutional Development, World Crisis and Developing Countries, Banking and Third World Debt: In Search of Solutions, World Banking and Finance: Cooperation Versus Conflict* (Praeger); with R. Lang and D. Vojnić, eds., *Essays on the Political Economy of Yugoslavia*; with Hui-Liany Tsai, *Money in Economic Systems*; with D. Dimitrijević, *Money and Finance in Yugoslavia: A Comparative Analysis* (Praeger).